COMMUNITY INITIATIVES IN
URBAN INFRASTRUCTURE

COMMUNITY INITIATIVES IN
URBAN INFRASTRUCTURE

A.P. Cotton, M. Sohail and W.K. Tayler

Water, Engineering and Development Centre
Loughborough University
1998

Water, Engineering and Development Centre
Loughborough University
Leicestershire
LE11 3TU UK

© Water, Engineering and Development Centre
Loughborough University 1998
Reprinted, 2019

ISBN 13 Paperback: 9780906055564
ISBN Library Ebook: 9781788532808
Book DOI: http://dx.doi.org/10.3362/9781788532808

A catalogue record for this book is available from the British Library.

Cotton, A.P. Sohail, A. Tayler, W.K (1998)
Community initiatives in urban infrastructure
WEDC, Loughborough University, UK.

This edition reprinted and distributed by Practical Action Publishing

Since 1974, Practical Action Publishing has published and disseminated books and information in support of international development work throughout the world. Practical Action Publishing trades only in support of its parent charity objectives and any profits are covenanted back to Practical Action
(Charity Reg. No. 247257, Group VAT Registration No. 880 9924 76).

This document is an output from a project funded by the UK Department for International Development (DFID) for the benefit of developing countries.
The views expressed are not necessarily those of DFID.

Layout by Karen Betts
Designed by Rod Shaw

Contents

Boxes

Annex

Photographs

Figure

Abbreviations

CBO	Community based organisation
CDC	Community Development Council
CMDA	Calcutta Metropolitan Development Authority (India)
CMG	Community Management Group
CSPU	Clean Settlements Project Unit (Sri Lanka)
ED	Engineering Department
FAUP	Faisalabad Area Upgrading Project (Pakistan)
ICTAD	Institute for Contractor Training & Development (Sri Lanka)
NGO	Non government organisation
NHDA	National Housing Development Authority (Sri Lanka)
OPP	Orangi Pilot Project (Pakistan)
PMU	Project Management Unit
PWD	Public Works Department
Rs	Rupees (local currency in India, Pakistan, Sri Lanka; £1~Rs55)
SKAA	Sindh Katchi Abadi Authority (Pakistan)
SO	Support Organisation
SoR	Schedule of Rates

Section 1

Introduction and background

About this manual

This manual presents the findings from Project R6264 *The Procurement of Infrastructure for Urban Low Income Communities* carried out by the Authors as part of the Technology, Development and Research Programme, Engineering Division, Department For International Development of the British Government. The purpose of the project is to investigate the extent and nature of the involvement of low income urban communities in the provision of their local infrastructure.

The purpose of this manual is to provide guidance for promoting increased involvement of low income urban communities in the procurement of neighbourhood (tertiary level) infrastructure. The contexts are several and varied including:

- upgrading works carried out by urban government;
- donor funded urban development programmes;
- programmes initiated by non government organisations (NGOs).

The manual aims to demonstrate the potential benefits to be gained from community partnered procurement. The readership for the manual are policy makers and professional staff of urban government, development agencies, non-government organisations, and small to medium enterprises involved with infrastructure procurement for low income urban communities. The content of the manual applies to those frequently occurring, low risk, routine small infrastructure works which characterise neighbourhood urban upgrading programmes and projects. We investigate cases relating to water supply, sanitation, drainage, access, paving, street and security lighting, solid waste removal, and community buildings. It is not applicable to complex, large, high risk and high hazard infrastructure projects.

The findings are based on the results of interviews and a review of literature, documents and project files on urban upgrading projects in

Pakistan, India and Sri Lanka. We are particularly grateful to the many government officials who so generously gave their time to us, and provided access to very detailed information on a wide range of both community-based infrastructure works and conventional procurement contracts.

The manual further develops the material contained in the earlier interim findings booklet, which was distributed informally in 1996. Its subject matter is timely in that the findings support the underlying themes of partnership implicit in the Habitat II city summit held in Istanbul in 1996.

Section 1 is about the manual itself, the background and scope of work; Section 2 outlines the process of infrastructure procurement; Section 3 briefly describes the cases which have been analysed, and refers to Annex 1 in which a detailed narrative and commentary are provided for each case. Section 4 discusses the main themes which emerge from the cases, and Section 5 offers guidance to actual and potential practitioners of community partnered procurement of neighbourhood infrastructure. This is the key section of the manual, and is identified by tinted pages. A literature review and listing of data sources will be available separately.

Background and scope of work

The urban population in most developing countries is increasing extremely rapidly. Conventional approaches have proved inadequate to meet the demand for shelter and services created by this rapid urban growth and this has led to a proliferation of informal, unimproved slum and squatter settlements where the inhabitants generally experience high levels of unemployment and underemployment. The United Nations Centre for Human Settlements suggests that between 40 per cent and 50 per cent of the population in many cities live in such settlements; according to present trends, this is likely to increase. The ability of government to provide infrastructure is already far outstripped by the inexorable increase in demand, so that the poorest and most vulnerable will continue to suffer from the lack of services and work opportunities.

This manual is about the *procurement* of infrastructure; that is, what mechanisms, both conventional and unconventional, government and non-government, have been adopted in efforts to deliver improved services. There is a noticeable lack of published material and guidance on the many different approaches which have been adopted in infrastructure procurement. We explore the mechanisms and processes of agreements, procedures and contracts that are the basis for implementation of infrastructure improvements for urban low income communities. The specific focus is on situations

2

where communities have taken a part in the planning and implementation of their neighbourhood infrastructure; this we term *community partnered procurement.*

This is one of the first investigations to look in detail at such community initiatives in the context of low income urban settlements and as such we have been primarily attempting to draw out a number of key themes and issues. Having established these key themes, it becomes apparent that in themselves they merit detailed investigation. A good example is the importance of the wider social and economic impacts of infrastructure; our work has shown this to be a key issue. However, detailed evaluation of these social and economic impacts has been outside the scope of this work, although we do indicate situations where we believe significant impacts have been achieved. This (and there are others) clearly requires separate further investigation.

The stimulation for this work has been the increasing international interest in promoting the participation of community groups in improving access to basic services at the household and neighbourhood levels. There is a substantial body of work addressing the issues of community participation and empowerment, which identifies barriers to increased community participation and suggests ideas and techniques for tackling the problems. These include the many currently popular tools related to participatory appraisal. Broadly speaking, this approaches matters internally, that is, the focus is on the cowmmunity, although appropriate institutional responses to increase the levels of participation are also considered.

However, with regard to community partnered procurement an additional set of barriers exist, namely the rules and procedures which urban government adopts in relation to procurement. These provide the framework within which urban government operates and the key question is whether existing rules and procedures offer any scope for the increased community participation which is being advocated. We therefore look in detail at why these procedures are used and how they work; we believe that understanding these processes is central to increasing the access of community groups to the funds and other resources of urban government.

There are cases where community partnered procurement operates outside the purview of urban government and we have included some examples . However, our main objective in writing this manual is to offer guidance as to how such local initiatives can be successfully integrated with urban government, as we believe that in this way it may be possible to see more responsive urban government and to increase the access which the urban poor have to resources for improved services.

Photograph 1:
Septic tank construction by community contractor in Colombo, Sri Lanka

Section 2

Infrastructure procurement

Procurement is the process of buying the goods, works or services, which in our case comprise the infrastructure and services described previously. In engineering terms, the works themselves are minor and usually of low cost, but are nevertheless complex to implement given the physical and social fabric of low income urban areas. We adopt the term *micro-contract* to refer to the countless number of small contracts for works which are the mainstay of urban improvement in South Asia. The contract value is typically less than £10 000, and the duration less than one year.

This project is based on work carried out in India, Pakistan and Sri Lanka where the legal framework was developed during the colonial period and is based on English law. During this time, the Public Works Department was responsible for implementation of building, public health, irrigation and general civil works. Detailed procedures were made to handle contemporary problems in the procurement of infrastructure; it is interesting to review their development, and to note that they were frequently amended in response to new situations. It was the then Superintending Engineers responsible for the works who suggested changes as and when they felt it necessary.

This contrasts sharply with the present day; in the post colonial period in Pakistan, for example, there have been few changes in almost fifty years. The situation has changed and continues to change, yet there is a lack of responsiveness to reflect this in the procurement procedures. This has led to an increasing gap between what is theoretically meant to happen and what actually happens on the ground, which leads in turn to inflexibility and lack of transparency.

At this stage, it is useful to consider briefly some of the basic concepts which will be central to the analysis of our findings. The *procedures* refer to the organized system within which projects are conceived, planned, and brought into being by urban government. The *contract* is a legally binding agreement between parties based on an offer by one party to do something (in our case to construct the infrastructure) in return for a consideration (that is, payment).

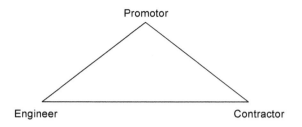

In urban government in South Asia, the most commonly used procedures for the procurement of infrastructure are those which lead to the award of contracts through competitive tender (Boxes 1, 2, 3). Their underlying objectives are concerned with ensuring *competition* which is viewed as a key factor in achieving the twin objectives of:

- *Accountability* in the spending of public money.
- *Transparency* in the steps of the decision-making processes.

In relation to the actual contracts, we need to focus on who is involved in a contract and what their various obligations are. The most commonly used engineering contracts recognize a 'triangle of actors': *Promoter; Engineer;* and *Contractor*.

A typical case in South Asia (and elsewhere) involves urban government letting a contract to a private sector contractor for the construction of infrastructure improvements. Urban government is the *promoter*; they have planned and designed the work, and are paying for it to be implemented. Urban government appoints an *Engineer*, who is usually in the full time employment of the relevant government department. It is rare for private sector consultants to fulfil this role for minor engineering works in South Asia. In accordance with the procedures laid down (see Box 4), a *contractor* is appointed to do the actual construction work.

The Engineer has the important role of ensuring that the interests of the promoter are met, and that the contractor is duly paid for his efforts. The promoter wants the best value for money and the contractor wants a good profit; whilst this can involve an enormous range of complex and contentious issues, satisfying the various interests often comes down to ensuring that a 'triangle of objectives' are met:

- *Cost:* has the work been completed within the costs agreed in the contract?
- *Quality*: has the work been done in accordance with what was specified?
- *Time*: has the work been satisfactorily completed within the time specified?

The traditionally accepted objectives of procurement procedures and contract documents are to ensure that works are executed at the minimum cost that is consistent with the need to achieve a product of acceptable quality within an acceptable timeframe. They do this by reducing uncertainty, which in turn is done by:

- clearly defining who is liable to take any risk that cannot be eliminated from the project;
- providing information on the work to be carried out so that all concerned are clear about what has to be done and what their role is in doing it.

Why community partnering?

Community groups and individual householders do not figure anywhere in the procedures, contracts and documentation used in these circumstances. It is assumed that they are passive consumers who are deemed to be satisfied if works are undertaken to the satisfaction of the promoter i.e. the concerned agency of urban government. Is this assumption justified, and if not what are the implications?

Normal government practice is based on the twin assumptions that a competitive market for infrastructure provision exists and that the best way to operate in this market is through competitive tendering procedures. The competitive market only works in practice if contractors act independently; this does not always happen in practice. Certain situations exist where contractors are concerned with stability rather than expanding their market share and maximising their profitability; the outcome is that they share out the available work between them. One consequence of this 'pooling' of work is that the assumption that conventional tendering procedures will produce the lowest cost work is not justified in practice.

The role of the Engineers in urban government is to ensure that objectives relating to cost, quality and time are achieved. As we report in Section 4 the objective which is most difficult to assess, and causes most concern, is the quality of the finished work. The fact is that neither they as supervisors nor the government as promoters are primary stakeholders with a strong motivation for ensuring that adequate work practices and standards are maintained.

It is questionable whether *value for money* is achieved; thus several reasons for promoting community partnering arise:

- Community members are directly affected by the way in which work is carried out and have a strong incentive to see that it is carried out properly.
- Resources can be channelled into the community rather than being siphoned off by outside contractors. Whereas conventional procurement

of infrastructure has a single benefit, the provision of the infrastructure itself, community partnering can double the benefits obtained from investment. Infrastructure is provided and employment opportunities and enterprises are created in the community.

- People are empowered to take more control of their own lives.
- Increased access to local knowledge is gained on such issues as the location of existing services and a reduction in the potential for disputes with community members in the course of work on site.

These arguments can be opposed on a number of grounds. Many government engineers are sceptical about the ability of community partnering to provide services to the required standard. Others fear that community partnering is likely to prove too complex to be much use in practice. Nevertheless, we have found that the involvement of community members and groups in the procurement of their local infrastructure is quite widespread but not, at present, great in scale. Consequently there are a number of questions to be addressed:

- If the procedures, contracts and documentation do not foresee a role for community members and groups, then how have existing community-based initiatives worked?
- To what extent do existing procedures create barriers to greater involvement of community groups as primary stakeholders ?
- How can these barriers be overcome in a way which is acceptable to urban government?
- Is there potential for increasing the scale of community partnering to a level at which it impacts on conditions in low income informal areas at a national scale?

Section 3

The cases

The case study material is presented as a series of boxes comprising a *narrative* which describes the pertinent facts of the situation, and a corresponding *commentary* which draws out significant points to be used as the basis for the discussion and guidelines. The narrative information is presented in considerable detail, as a cornerstone of this work is to understand the practical detail of how community partnered procurement has operated. As this requires considerable space, the boxes are located in Annex 1.

The following can be found in Annex 1:

- Boxes 1 to 6 give the background to government procedures for the procurement of infrastructure, which are in general terms common to the three study countries.
- Boxes 7 to 18 concern the different roles and responsibilities assumed by the various partners.
- Boxes 19 to 25 focus on issues related to processes and contracting which involve communities.
- Boxes 26 to 30 look at different forms of agreement and contract which have been used.

Photograph 2:
Micro contractors improving secondary drainage, Cuttack, India

Photograph 3:
Community management of neighbourhood drain construction in Colombo, Sri Lanka

Section 4

Lessons from the cases

Roles and responsibilities

One of the most interesting findings is the wide variety of ways in which community groups become involved in the development of local infrastructure and service provision. They take on and adapt to many differing roles, ranging from informal advisers, through to formally appointed micro-contractors with legally binding contracts to construct the works, for which they receive cash payment. We have found examples of community groups participating in all of the roles within the contractual triangle described in Section 1. For example:

- Community as promoter (Boxes 7 to 9).
- Community as engineer (Boxes 10 to 13).
- Community as contractor (Boxes 14 to 18).

These are reflected by the following examples of detailed activities:

- Participation in the identification, planning and design of improvements (Boxes 7, 8, 9).
- Involvement in the supervision and quality control of works undertaken by a government contractor appointed through the standard tendering procedures (Box 10).
- Use of waged local labour in Departmental Works; materials are procured either by the community or by the government department (Box 13).
- Use of community labour engaged and paid through labour-only contracts (Box 15).
- Community-based labour employed by a private sector contractor appointed under the tender-contract system (Box 14).
- Entrustment of works by negotiation, where the community group has management control of the construction and chooses whether it uses local labour or hires in labour from outside (Box 16).

- Formation of local societies with the view to undertaking work in a number of slum communities (Box 18).
- Capacity building and skills upgrading of micro-contractors and community groups with the assistance of NGOs (Boxes 7, 8).
- Improvements financed partly by the community and partly by government (Box 9).
- Improvements which are fully financed internally by the community who develop procedures specific to their needs without any government involvement but with NGO support (Boxes 7, 8).

It is therefore particularly important not to typecast peoples' involvement in terms of the traditional 'community-labour' approach. In fact it cannot be assumed that urban low income communities will do the construction labouring work themselves. We have found evidence of community groups engaging in sophisticated sub contracting and management (Boxes 7, 18 and 19). It can be more complex if the community becomes both Promoter and Contractor (Box 7). On the other hand, some communities are mainly interested in the opportunities for waged employment as a means of boosting their very low incomes.

Operation and maintenance of urban infrastructure has traditionally been an area of serious neglect. Recognising community groups as primary stakeholders can introduce additional complications, which may partly be reflected by confusion over *ownership:*

- as a developmental concept relating to processes which involve community groups as primary stakeholders;
- as a legal concept in relation to the assets created.

Disputes over responsibility arose when the departmental works procedure was used in collaboration with a NGO and community groups in Karachi (Box 13), despite the fact that the implementation of the works was successful. The importance of clarity during negotiations is brought out by the rather complex situation in a CSPU contract in Sri Lanka (Box 23). The CSPU is a project unit within a government department, and is the partial (80 per cent) promoter; it argues that it cannot enter into maintenance contracts 'because of the temporary nature (of the CSPU)'. No arrangements with other agencies are in place, and it is tacitly assumed that the community based organisation (CBO) is responsible for maintenance.

This contrasts with the approach in Calcutta (Box 10); although the community only has a role as informal advisers, the promoter (the Urban Development Authority) ensures as part of the negotiations that arrangements are in place for handover to the maintaining authority (the Municipal Corporation).

All the indications are that, contrary to the views of a number of professionals, urban infrastructure at the local (tertiary) level is not 'too complicated' for ordinary people to get to grips with. Urban infrastructure *is* complex, but nevertheless community groups in different situations demonstrate their ability to play a positive role. The key point to emerge is that there is no single identifiable role model for *Community Partnered Procurement.*

Government procedures: a surprising amount of scope

Given the complexity of roles and responsibilities which we have found to exist in community partnered procurement, it is necessary to explore in detail how these initiatives can link into urban government through the confines of their procedures. Local government procurement procedures are described in Boxes 1 and 2. The most significant finding (Box 2) is that some of these procedures allow a surprising degree of flexibility. Negotiation is acceptable, and it is even possible to offer works at a discount to certain registered societies and cooperatives.

In Pakistan (Boxes 13 and 25) we have a case where Departmental Works Procedure (Box 2) has been adopted on a large scale with the involvement of a NGO. External works have been procured in this way, with the subsequent result that community groups financed and installed internal lane-level works. The motivation and backing for this approach comes from the top official in the organisation in response to problems with poor quality, cost overruns and time overruns which plagued work carried out under the routine tender contract system. This is one of many indications of an inherent danger in the way the tender-contract system is used, whereby it offers cheapness as opposed to value for money.

However, it is clear that a distinction needs to be drawn between what is done *as a matter of routine* and what *could be done* within existing procedures. The routine is to use competitive tender to award the contract to the lowest bidder because this is believed to ensure *de facto* the objective of value for money. Adopting other procedures, which are by definition non-routine, is theoretically acceptable, but few engineers are willing to subject themselves to the consequent need for justifying such a decision.

It is usual that only enlisted contractors are permitted to tender for work with urban government (Box 4). This preliminary screening process is designed to weed out unsuitable candidates. However, the problem is that the material and financial constraints which enlistment imposes means that community groups are excluded from the most common routine procurement mechanism. Therefore we need to look for alternatives in the early stages of the community groups acting as contractors.

We also observe the officials of urban government negotiating satisfactory arrangements with the community along the lines of the systems (which do not involve government) operating in Orangi (Box 7). The outcome is of mutual benefit firstly to the community through empowerment and income generation and secondly to urban government who get better value for money and better quality work (Box 18). Yet these officials are struggling to provide file notes and documentary support which mirror the formally sanctioned procedures, but which in themselves are of little significance to the success of the partnership with the community (Boxes 16 and 17). An important issue for these officials is not the cost or the quality *per se*, but an ability to prove *in accordance with procedure* that the cost was advantageous to government; this is essential to protect themselves from the unwelcome attention of the Central Audit and Account Organisation.

We believe that this reluctance to do anything other than accept the lowest tender, regardless of the appropriateness or likely outcome, is due in no small part to the system of financial auditing which has developed. The following points are central to this vexing problem:

- The money flowing in and out of government departments at all levels is controlled by the Central Audit and Account Organisation; this is a powerful organisation in terms of the power and influence it wields.
- It can (and sometimes does) act in a malign way; officials can be called to account for the minutest deviation from arcane rules. Government Engineers are vested with the authority of sanctioning different stages of the procurement process. They can subsequently be held personally liable for overspending, and in extreme cases face the possibility of personal ruin.
- The key concern is to *demonstrate* value for money and that rules have been followed to the letter. This does not necessarily equate with probity and efficiency in the spending of public money.
- Audit requirements, or more accurately fear of the audit on the part of middle and junior ranking officials, can be taken as a governing factor in the use of what we describe as 'non routine' procedure in the public sector. In general, they require the written backing of the equivalent of the Chief Executive before adopting non-routine procedures.

The problem is that procedures designed to try to eliminate malpractice also stifle genuine innovation. Without the explicit backing of top officials, few middle ranking engineers are prepared to adopt anything other than the competitive tender; the risks are simply not worth taking.

The Engineer is of crucial importance in community partnered procurement because of the delegated authority vested in the position. Any changes designed to promote community partnering as a means of procurement of works undertaken with public money must not increase their personal risk.

Accountability and transparency

We have recognised limitations of the tender contract system and tried to identify some of the practical (as opposed to theoretical) reasons for its widespread adoption to the exclusion of almost everything else. The procurement of infrastructure is complex and expensive regardless of how or by whom it is done. It is therefore important to see how other procedures which offer more scope for community partnered procurement can satisfy the twin goals of transparency and accountability; the means of achieving this could hardly be more diverse.

Whose money is it?

We have encountered three different situations regarding sources of finance:

1. Government money is used to finance the works; community groups are paid for services which they provide. This injects money into the local economy.
2. Government money is not involved; the finance is raised internally by community groups and existing money recirculates in the local economy.
3. Split funding with contributions from government and community groups.

The source of finance is the single most important factor in relation to the procedures and rules which are adopted for infrastructure procurement. If government finance is involved, whether in full or in part, its rules and procedures which run into volumes of written words must be adhered to (Boxes 1 and 2). This includes money from other sources such as bilateral agencies which is channelled through government. We have seen what a powerful influence audit and accounting arrangements can have on the behaviour of Engineers.

Negotiation between urban government and a community group to agree a price for the work resulted in a lower price than conventional tendering would have produced, a fact which is very important for the officials of urban government in justifying the process (Boxes 15 and 16).

If the finance is raised by the community, then they are at liberty to define and use whatever mechanisms they feel confident with (Box 7). They develop systems which have minimal written documentation and are enforceable by social pressure and 'private ordering' rather than 'court ordering' Relatively little reliance is placed on the written word, and trust between the partners is the key.

In Faisalabad, Pakistan (Box 9) a hybrid situation with joint financing has arisen. Thus on the same micro contract, the community groups on the one hand and government agencies on the other require different procedures to satisfy their own perceptions of transparency and accountability. A lot of confidence building is necessary if residents are to be encouraged to deposit money in a joint account with government, as in this case. No formal contracts are on file for the construction of the lane sewers.

However, the FAUP procurement strategy for lane sewers has been successful as measured by cost and quality, which are themselves key objectives for *government* procurement. The irony is that if the FAUP system were subject to scrutiny by the government's Central Audit and Account Organisation, in all probability questions would be raised about the procedures used to demonstrate value for money. Here, then, is the archetypal problem whereby successful community partnering develops on the fringes of urban government; yet looming on the horizon is the apparent inability of government to assimilate these successful processes and procedures.

How are decisions reached?

In the routine tender-contract procedures, the relationships between promoter, engineer and contractor are clearly defined and understood by the parties involved. Everything is set out in the contract and its accompanying documentation. When problems arise, formal mechanisms specified in the contract for dispute resolution are invoked. One of the most striking facts about the formal contracts which are run by the engineers of urban government is the high standard of documentation and record keeping, which in some cases such as the CMDA in Calcutta is exemplary (Box 10). In these files are the records which demonstrate that the concerned officials have followed the rules and procedures (Box 1). Some day, they might have to answer to procedural queries raised by the Central Audit and Accounts Department and, by means of these files, will be called to account for their actions.

This contrasts with many of the cases in which community groups are involved together with urban government; a continuous process of negotiation and dialogue is more in evidence. In a number of cases this is because the parties are working in a genuinely experimental situation in which there are no hard and fast rules. Informal negotiation emerges as a key element in successful initiatives involving community groups; it provides mechanisms for agreeing costs and resolving disputes. The real business of dispute resolution in Cuttack, India (Box 17) was done by negotiation; some of the documents and file notes have the appearance of 'after the event' formalities.

The FAUP (Box 9) set up its own project approval committee, whose purpose is to grant sanction to specific project activities. Its membership includes officials from other urban government agencies. These members (quite appropriately) questioned the legitimacy of the actions of the committee.

An interesting contrast is provided by a case in Pakistan (Box 7) where people get on with things themselves, with the support of a NGO, but without the involvement of urban government. Agreements between residents and micro-contractors are negotiated; there is no written contract because it would serve no useful purpose. The system is well established, and disputes are resolved through negotiation without recourse to any written agreement. A cost estimate is prepared on the basis of market rates and in a form which is useful to the residents in managing the work; this contrasts with standard government procedure (Box 6) where even for a formal contractor the official methods of cost estimation are not helpful in managing the work.

This draws attention to the importance of the local micro-contractors who play a crucial role, but who are rarely the focus of discussion. These masons, carpenters and plumbers provide the skilled labour input and often manage the micro-contracts for local improvement works. Their importance has emerged in Pakistan (Boxes 7 and 13), in Sri Lanka (Box 19) and in India (Box 16). The ability and experience of the micro-contractors provide a crucial link in the chain leading to a successful outcome. They are key players in any negotiations about price, and their ability and skills are important determinants of the quality of the work produced.

Performance of community partnered procurement

It is necessary to review how the performance of these relatively limited experiences compares with the conventional tender contract systems. As a starting point we attempt some comparisons with the traditional performance measures of procurement contracts, namely time, cost, and quality of work. In order to achieve credibility, community partnered procurement needs to measure up at least as well as the tender contract system on these traditional performance indicators.

Cost
The use of informal negotiation to agree prices and resolve operational problems is an important feature of community partnering. However, with regard to agreeing a price, there needs to be a basis around which the negotiations can proceed. Cost estimates based on the existing Schedule of

Rates (Box 6) has been used in Sri Lanka and India; this creates problems for community groups unless estimations based on market rates are also made. The market testing approach has also been tried (Box 16).

The specific evidence we have uncovered from a preliminary analysis of 390 micro contracts in India and Pakistan and Sri Lanka indicates that the final price for community partnered works is lower than for the conventional tender contract system. The mean cost growth (that is, the ratio of actual completion cost to the tendered cost) for 239 cases of conventionally procured works using the tender contract system is 1.0, whereas for 151 community partnered procurement arrangements the mean value is 0.90. The key point is that this outcome is achieved through negotiating down the rates for the work. This has been officially recognised in the Treasury Circulars of the Government of Sri Lanka (Boxes 20 and 21). Whilst these mean values mask considerable variations, it is interesting to observe the overall control on costs which is being achieved.

Time

The required completion time is specified in the conventional tender contract system; penalties such as liquidated damages can be invoked, although interviews with engineers suggest that in practice this is hardly ever done on micro contracts. The mean time growth (that is, the ratio of the actual lapse time of the construction to the duration stated in the contract) for 239 cases of conventionally procured works using the tender contract system is 1.5, whereas for 151 community partnered procurement arrangements the mean value is 1.9. It is not clear why this is so large compared with the cost growth reported above; the implication is that cost growth is a serious concern to supervising engineers and they control it in order to avoid getting into personal difficulty. There does not seem to be a similar pressure to control time overrun. In community partnered works, we have found little concern with completion time, to the extent that it is often not mentioned at all in the agreements. In Sri Lanka, the NHDA guidelines for community based works contain a liquidated damages clause, although officials comment that they would never intend invoking it. The impression is that with community partnering arrangements there is sufficient incentive available for the work to be completed without the need for invoking penalties.

The detailed findings of the investigations into time and cost growth in micro contracts will be published separately.

Quality

It is difficult to measure quality of work in a quantitative way, and to date we have only found subjective opinions. However, some of these are quite telling; for example Box 13 describes how poor quality of work was a key contributing factor in abandoning the tender contract system in favour of Departmental Works. Supervision of work by community groups is reported to be successful (Boxes 8 and 10); this benefited from setting down a clear structure for their involvement. The Sri Lankan experience reports improved quality. There are no reported cases of the quality of the work being worse with community partnering. It is nevertheless important to note that some of the experiences, for example Boxes 7 and 18, are the outcome of an approach which has taken some considerable time and experimentation to come to fruition; the mistakes made along the way are less frequently reported. We conjecture that the time overrun described above is likely to have a deleterious effect on quality. The cost of materials rises with time (quite dramatically in some case study cities); if the total contract cost is closely controlled (as is the case) and material costs have risen, then it is conceivable that the contractor absorbs this by reducing the quality of work to below that specified.

Clearly, cost and quality are closely interrelated. The routine application of government procedure almost without fail selects the cheapest bid, which in certain circumstances compromises the quality of the final product. An apparently minor incident in Faisalabad (Box 9) draws the conflict between cost and quality into sharp focus. The community group stated that it could not afford the high specification for concrete sewer pipes which the government specification requires. The government therefore states its position that it cannot commit its share of the funds; the community responds that in that case there will be no project, period. The community view prevailed in this case, and the sewer project went ahead.

This is symptomatic of a highly controversial argument about levels of service and design standards which has to be faced up to. Traditionally, planners and engineers develop infrastructure schemes based on predefined notions of what is best. These are reflected in the Codes of Practice and Standards which are often unrealistically high and inappropriate for the circumstances. In Faisalabad, people want a service which is *within their reach*, built to standards which are appropriate for the circumstances, rather than something which somebody else has decreed is better for them. This, in fact, is no more than the sound approach which a supplier of consumer goods takes; develop products which customers want and will buy. Standards can no longer be 'absolute' and applied in a vacuum without reference to the customers.

Wider benefits of community partnered procurement

Local infrastructure improvements are usually predicated on benefits to environmental health. Our investigations lead us to believe that community partnered procurement of infrastructure may enable much wider objectives (in addition to the traditional environmental health benefits) to be achieved through *addressing the poverty agenda* in relation to:

- the participation process as a means of offering empowerment and greater control to households and community groups;
- employment opportunities leading to income generation for low income groups who are paid for undertaking work associated with government funded infrastructure improvements;
- small enterprise development as local micro-contractors develop and exploit the niches created;
- other benefits to the local micro-economy such as increased business for building materials suppliers.

The Sri Lankan experience (Boxes 18 and 19) demonstrate community partnered procurement injecting substantial amounts of new money into the local economy of low income communities in a way which is not welfare-orientated. Different community groups respond in different ways, and micro-contracting enterprises develop; two community groups undertook 32 per cent of the work in the NHDA community contracts in Sri Lanka. The pilot projects in Cuttack and Cochin, India (Boxes 14 to 17) are showing good potential. In these cases, government is either providing or acting as a channel for the funding. In situations where communities themselves fund the work internally (Boxes 7 to 9), existing money is recirculating. However, whilst direct income generation is not a benefit here, there is evidence of sustainable enterprise development through the strengthening of local micro-contractors.

There is evidence of greater empowerment and control in all the cases we reviewed. This is particularly noticeable where there has been the involvement of a strong NGO (Boxes 7, 8, 12 and 13). Increased networking between slum communities is another important impact (Box 12). There are also a number of relatively minor instances which are nevertheless important indicators of future potential. For example in Cuttack, India, (Box 17) the community management group soon ceases to be a mere passive receiver of ideas and instructions from the project management unit. The file reveals an increasingly formal tone to their communications and they developed sufficient confidence to question the actions of government through the official channels.

Some of these additional benefits, in particular income generation and enterprise development, are not necessarily area-based; experience from Pakistan and Sri Lanka supports this, although a more detailed impact analysis which is beyond the scope of the current work is desirable. Through community partnering it is possible to look beyond the physical slum into different groups of the urban poor, where the skilled and unskilled labour pool necessary to contribute to the infrastructure improvements almost certainly exists. Implementing works through community partnering provides opportunities for targeting interventions in a way which integrates into wider strategies of urban poverty reduction.

On the limited evidence available, the case for community partnering in its broadest sense is strong. Not only does it apparently compete favourably in terms of the traditional contractual performance measures of cost and quality (although the time growth appears greater) it offers a whole range of other potential benefits which can be targeted at low income groups to assist their empowerment and improve their economic conditions. The problem is the lack of a framework and tools which can be used to capture the diversity of what appears to be happening in order to assess these potential impacts.

Constraints on community partnered procurement

Two distinct situations exist in the cases explored:

1. Community based actions outside of government which are supported by NGOs.
2. Community based actions within the framework of a government programme.

Both have similar problems in terms of developing a participation process. However, in the first case, there is more or less total freedom in terms of subsequent processes and procedures to move ahead with actions (in our cases, infrastructure initiatives) which are outcomes of the participation process (Box 7). In the second case, an additional set of problems stems from attempts to develop these subsequent actions within the context of urban government. This creates problems for community groups and government officials alike. A recurring difficulty is the lack of capacity of the middle ranking engineers within urban government, who have a central role in community partnering schemes.

Considerable transaction costs are incurred by all involved . Community groups invest a lot of their time during the development of the participation process, and in gaining sufficient confidence to become involved in infrastructure procurement. This has been recognised by earlier work and can be seen as part of a wider process of empowerment.

What has been less clearly stated is that during the early stages of implementation, a lot of effort also has to be put in by government officials, in complete disproportion to the engineering work in hand. The processes of explaining the concepts, assessing the capacity of community groups, entering into negotiations and providing technical support during construction, are all time consuming activities. This is evident in India (Boxes 16 and 17). Once the initial stages are over and the programme develops further, serious time constraints arise for the officials (Box 13). This is particularly important for government engineers who usually have a quota of work (in financial terms) which they are expected to handle in a particular year. However, in Sri Lanka, which has the most extensive experience of community contracting, once systems were in place and operating, there was not much difference in supervision time between using conventional or community contractors (Box 19).

Involving support organisations, whether private sector commercial or NGO, as intermediaries clearly has advantages to offer in this respect. However, it is important to keep the level of support in context with the work in hand, even though there is clearly a need for a lot of support at the outset of a new programme. This reflects in the management costs, which may be considerable especially where international agencies are involved. (Box 9). Even when local support organisations are involved, these costs can be considerable. In one situation in Sri Lanka, consultancy costs paid to a NGO amounted to 200 per cent of the contract cost for the actual infrastructure works (Boxes 23 and 24). It is therefore important that monitoring and evaluation procedures take these costs into account as part of the overall impact assessment.

An important benefit of the tender contract system is that urban government buys in the management capacity of the contractor as well as his construction capacity (Box 10). Under Departmental Works Procedure (Boxes 2 and 13), engineers and technicians experience difficulties in devoting time to the supervision of labour and in ensuring that the correct materials are available when required. The financial capacity of the contractor is important because government operates on a cost reimbursement basis; this means that any group acting in the capacity of a contractor must have access to 'money up front' in order to purchase materials and pay the labour force. This created problems in Sri Lanka and in India, where there were cases of government officials taking out advances in their own name in order to provide pre-financing to community groups. This situation is neither sustainable nor desirable.

The quality of work resulting from community partnering arrangements is generally perceived to be better than using conventional contractors. However, good quality work is not an automatic outcome; community groups and micro-contractors alike need some form of on-the-job training and skills upgrading. The apparently simple task of placing earth fill to form access ways initially failed because of lack of experience and inadequate supervision (Box 15). It is not reasonable to entrust community groups (or anybody else for that matter) with tasks of which they have no previous experience, and expect a quality product. In Pakistan (Boxes 7 and 8) NGO support for the capacity building of community groups and micro contractors has been a very important component of success.

There is a strong tendency for government engineering departments to refuse to adopt any infrastructure which has not been constructed by themselves. This indicates a need for dialogue with the relevant government departments from an early stage (Box 9).

Institutionalising community partnered procurement

Adopting non routine procedures clearly creates problems for government officials. We have seen evidence of their discomfort and concern, largely as a result of fear of the Audit and Account Organisation. Only in Sri Lanka do we see a national organisational culture developing which is making positive efforts to include these alternative ways of working into the mainstream. Also in Pakistan the Sindh Katchi Abadi Authority has modified procedures (Box 25).

The Government of Sri Lanka conducted a thorough review of the system of 'awarding negotiated contracts to approved societies'; this included auditing of a large number of contracts. The letters and Treasury Circulars contain some of the most important innovations which we have found in relation to government attitude to community based work (Boxes 20 to 22). They have assimilated lessons of the 'community contracting' experience, in particular the crucial role which negotiation plays; the rules now specifically grant an exemption for awarding work to 'approved societies' through negotiation *without resorting to public tender*. This recognises the fact that very advantageous cost terms can be obtained by negotiation with community groups. Our findings support this conclusion. This exemption should free officials from the continual worry about how to demonstrate value for money without a call for tenders, and should give them more opportunity to concentrate on issues central to community partnering negotiations.

The fact that the system has passed through the Audit and Account Organisation is significant and offers security to practitioners. As new processes develop, and depending on the local circumstances, there may be advantages in informally contacting the auditors and obtaining an opinion, rather than trying to disguise what is happening.

The NHDA of Sri Lanka has issued supporting guidelines for assigning small contracts to community groups (Box 22). These are important not only in themselves, but because they advertise the fact that assigning work to community groups is part of the standard procedure of the organisation. This is crucial to the way in which officials behave and should increase their confidence in adopting new approaches. Much of the experience we report from within government concerns small groups or individuals who have to some extent gone out on a limb in order to promote community partnering; there is a distinct sense of struggling against the prevailing flow. The existence of clear procedural rules and guidelines indicates the commitment of the organisation to these new approaches.

Photograph 4:
Community contractors construct a concrete lane, Cuttack, India

Section 5

Guidelines for community
partnered procurement

The purpose of this section is to provide guidance on the involvement of community groups in infrastructure procurement. We view partnering in procurement as fitting in to a larger picture of community based activities which are either being promoted as part of a programme involving urban government, or are part of local initiatives facilitated and supported by NGOs or other support organisations . We therefore assume that community development activities are in place, and that the following guidelines will be used to build on the outcomes of existing community mobilisation and the development of participation within the community group. The issues raised are derived from the cases presented in Section 3; hence these are quite specific in that they relate to infrastructure procurement interventions, albeit in a way which attempts to take a much wider view of the impact of procurement.

These guidelines do not propose a step by step methodology leading to guaranteed success; we are dealing with a process, and local circumstances will dictate the precise details. This section is structured around the range of possible roles and responsibilities adopted by the partners, with the guidelines presented as a series of discrete text boxes (Boxes G1 to G16). Cross reference is made within these text boxes to the cases presented in section 3; however, note that these cross references serve to illustrate problems as much as solutions. The flow chart (Figure 5.1) guides the reader through the sequence of text boxes.

Boxes G1 to G7 give guidance in relation to a set of generally applicable key issues. These include the concepts underlying the approach of community partnered procurement which places community groups at the centre of activities, rather than at the periphery as is common in conventional procurement. Successful partnerships can develop between different actors according to local circumstances. It is important to perceive the actual procurement of infrastructure as part of a much longer process, the key to which is participatory planning of improvements to urban services. It is during this process that the potential roles which community groups can play in procurement will develop; the key outcome of the participatory planning is the generation of one or more micro contracts. Whilst we have found that community groups have become involved in quite complex procurement arrangements, it is important to be realistic about the scope of the work and we characterise typical works which have been successful. Clearly, the identification and adoption of specific roles is dependent upon the capacity to undertake associated activities and we suggest certain indicators. However, this opens up a whole field which is outside the scope of this work, namely how to support and build on the existing capacity so that community groups are able to grow into new and different roles. The organisational status of community groups, whether informal or registered, is significant if urban government is a partner.

In Box G8, we identify the source of finance for infrastructure improvements as an important signpost to the various procedural routes which are available; from this point onwards, the guidelines identify particular text boxes with specific roles.

The *Community as Full Promoter* pays the total cost of the assets (infrastructure) created. Whilst there are no formal procedural requirements, guidance on preparing to enter into an agreement and on selecting a contract is suggested. Should a written contract be adopted, this leads to further guidance points on negotiation, documentation and sample agreements.

The *Community as Partial Promoter* pays some but not all of the costs of the assets. We have found that the non-community contribution comes either from or via urban government, even if it is channelled through an intermediary. In this case the guidelines follow government procedure in relation to project approval and procurement mechanisms and include estimating the cost of the works and access to finance. The preparations for entering into agreements are crucial; the guidance offered here is in common with other potential community roles, as are selecting and negotiating a contract. We have also identified a number of issues which are relevant when construction work is underway.

The *Community as Engineer* is involved in supervision, monitoring and quality control of the construction, in addition to contributing to the engineering related activities during participatory planning. The guidelines on preparing to enter into an agreement are particularly relevant in that responsibilities and delegated authorities need to be clear, especially if the other parties are urban government and micro contractors who are used to working only in a conventional situation. The guidelines on selecting and negotiating contracts and documentation incorporate the need to make these responsibilities clear.

The *Community as Contractor* undertakes the provision and management of construction in accordance with the contract. Urban government will almost certainly be a partner, so the guidance on selecting appropriate procedures is extremely important given the potentially high risks which community groups may take. This is also reflected in the guidelines on cost estimation and access to finance. The importance of the guidance on preparing to enter agreements also applies here. The guidance on selecting and negotiating contracts and documentation is supplemented by a sample agreement, and the examples of actual contracts which are presented should also be referred to (Boxes 27 – 30).

Photograph 5:
PMU staff offer technical support to community contractors, Cuttack, India

Figure 5.1. Using the guidelines

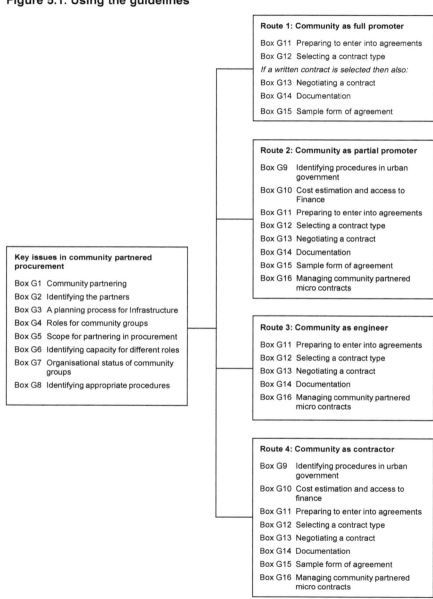

Route 1: Community as full promoter

Box G11 Preparing to enter into agreements

Box G12 Selecting a contract type

If a written contract is selected then also:

Box G13 Negotiating a contract

Box G14 Documentation

Box G15 Sample form of agreement

Route 2: Community as partial promoter

Box G9 Identifying procedures in urban government

Box G10 Cost estimation and access to Finance

Box G11 Preparing to enter into agreements

Box G12 Selecting a contract type

Box G13 Negotiating a contract

Box G14 Documentation

Box G15 Sample form of agreement

Box G16 Managing community partnered micro contracts

Key issues in community partnered procurement

Box G1 Community partnering

Box G2 Identifying the partners

Box G3 A planning process for Infrastructure

Box G4 Roles for community groups

Box G5 Scope for partnering in procurement

Box G6 Identifying capacity for different roles

Box G7 Organisational status of community groups

Box G8 Identifying appropriate procedures

Route 3: Community as engineer

Box G11 Preparing to enter into agreements

Box G12 Selecting a contract type

Box G13 Negotiating a contract

Box G14 Documentation

Box G16 Managing community partnered micro contracts

Route 4: Community as contractor

Box G9 Identifying procedures in urban government

Box G10 Cost estimation and access to finance

Box G11 Preparing to enter into agreements

Box G12 Selecting a contract type

Box G13 Negotiating a contract

Box G14 Documentation

Box G15 Sample form of agreement

Box G16 Managing community partnered micro contracts

Box G1. Community partnering

The concept of *Community Partnering* embraces the variety of roles and responsibilities described in Section 2. It reflects the continued involvement of people with the planning, implementation and sustenance of local infrastructure and service improvements, and with income generation, enterprise development and skills training. This implies:

- full acceptance of the urban poor as primary stakeholders in local infrastructure provision;

- developing longer term more open-ended relationships, encompassing joint

  financing, planning, design, implementation, hand over and maintenance;

- promoting co-operation both formally and informally with government agencies and NGOs;

- wider targeting of the urban poor, rather than solely area-based dwellers in specific slums, as local inhabitants do not necessarily carry out improvement works themselves because of lack of both time and relevant skills.

Photograph 6:
Community management of sewer construction, Faisalabad, Pakistan

29

Box G2. Identifying the partners

- Community Groups.

- Urban Government.

- Non Government Organisations (NGOs).

- Local micro contractors.

There are clearly a number of ways in which partnerships can form between a community group and one or more of these actors. The key point is that there is no sense in prescribing who the partners should be; our evidence does not point to a single universal model, but suggests that it is the highly specific local context and circumstances which determines the best way forwards.

The role of urban government can be either direct or indirect. In the latter case, we have found cases where a NGO is appointed as an intermediary either directly on behalf of government, or on behalf of international donor agencies who themselves are working through government. We treat these situations as if urban government were directly involved.

Box G3. A planning process for infrastructure

The process of developing partnerships will start well before it is time to consider procurement activities. Unless community groups have been involved throughout the planning process it is unlikely that partnering in procurement will be successful. The following summary outlines steps in a participatory infrastructure planning approach.

- Consultations between partners to ascertain demand for improved services.

- Outline options for service improvements.

- Estimate indicative costs of different options.

- Consider the operation and maintenance implications of different options.

- Explore alternatives for financing infrastructure improvements.

- Select options for service improvements.

- Preliminary planning of infrastructure improvements.

- Identify micro contracts associated with the infrastructure plan.

Box G4. Roles for community groups

We have already commented on the variety and complexity of roles and responsibilities which community groups have taken on. External factors, particularly the extent and source of funding for infrastructure improvements have an important influence on the eventual roles adopted. In summary the following roles can be played either fully or partially:

Promoter/Client (Boxes 7, 8, 9)
• Partial or full financiers and managers of the assets created.

Engineer (Boxes 10, 11, 12)
• Involved in information provision, planning, design, monitoring and evaluation.

Contractor (Boxes 14, 15, 16, 17, 18)
• Labour supplier only (Boxes 14, 15).

• Labour and material suppliers (Box 16).

• Sub-contractor.

• Main contractor (Boxes 17, 18).

Box G5. Scope for partnering in procurement

We have now reached the key stage for developing a specific procurement strategy.

• The project/programme generates one or more micro contracts.

However, not all work is suitable for community partnered procurement; potential micro contracts need the following characteristics:

• Low risk, low hazard.

• Technically and managerially straightforward.

• Labour intensive.

• Not requiring highly specialised skills.

Some examples of typical works:

• Excavation (pipeline/sewer trenching, foundations).

• Earth and gravel filling (land reclamation, road formation).

• Simple masonry and concrete work (paving, single storey buildings, latrines, solid waste bins, water points, bathing enclosures, manholes).

• Pipe laying and plumbing (water reticulation, sewer lines, water points, manholes).

Box G6. Identifying capacity for different roles

Assigning mutually agreed roles amongst the different partners requires an assessment of each other's capacity to perform. Capacities in different areas are required.

- *Technical:* for community as construction contractor or engineer; urban government and/or NGOs as technical facilitators.

- *Financial:* for community and/or NGOs as total or partial promoters.

- *Managerial:* important for all partners and all roles.

There are important indicators to look for and potential activities to support within the community when considering different roles. For example:

- Residents who are experienced skilled construction workers; they play a key role in managing the construction process as well as contributing their artisan skills. They have the potential to act as trainers and demonstrators.

- Residents who operate as local entrepreneurs surviving in the local economy, but not necessarily in construction, can assist in organising the business development side.

- The ability to raise and handle money for collective activity; the urban poor can be good financiers. Community groups may not have experience of bank transaction; individual or joint personal accounts are easier to open than company accounts.

- The management of past and existing community based activities. How transparent is the decision making process; are disadvantaged groups part of the decisions or are they simply passive listeners?

- Can it be demonstrated that a decision was taken in the good faith if it goes wrong. This could be facilitated by keeping a record of the factors and the risks considered at the time of the decision making.

- Evidence of financial and management accountability in community groups/NGOs: can expenditure be traced.

Note: Some traditional indicators used in evaluating the capacities of conventional registered contractors may *not* be relevant when considering the community as a potential contractor. Examples include: evidence of financial strength from bank accounts; numbers of people permanently employed; inventory of plants and tools owned.

Box G7. The organisational status of community groups

The status of community groups and community based organisations (CBOs) is relevant if urban government is involved. Broadly speaking, there are mechanisms through which community groups can become registered and thereby be legally recognised by government in its dealings with them. This applies to NGOs as well. The situation becomes more complex if the community group has no clear legal status; it may be difficult for urban government to procure services from neighbourhood level informal organisations. In the latter case there are a number of possible approaches:

*   Keep the relationship on a personal level; the legal status of the organisation will not arise so long as urban government or private sector organisations can enter into a contract with a person or group of people (Box 13).

*   See if the informal status can be upgraded through local urban bye-laws as was done with Community Development Councils in Sri Lanka.

*   Treat the relationship as a special case or experiment and obtain special approval from the appropriate authorities in urban government (Boxes 9, 13).

*   Keep a direct relationship between urban government and the community group out of the design of the project and use intermediaries such as NGOs (Boxes 8, 12).

The problem is that registering community groups can involve lengthy bureaucratic processes. However, the advantages lie in having the status to develop relationships with urban government and to develop small enterprises.

Box G8. Identifying appropriate procedures

The source of funds for the infrastructure improvements has an important influence on the procedures which are available and the flexibility of the approaches adopted.

*   If urban government is not involved, it is not necessary to follow formal procedures, and matters may progress on the basis of verbal (i.e. unwritten) agreements. However, if there is the prospect of linking in to the resources of urban government in the future, it is a good idea to mirror their procedures so that it becomes possible to slot into a programme as and when appropriate. The procedures themselves are logical and if followed in the spirit of partnering will help to maintain transparency and accountability; the difference may be the extent to which written records are kept.

*   If part or all of the finance originates or is channelled through urban government, follow their procedures for obtaining the necessary sanctions and award of the micro contract. This also holds true for projects or programmes which work through NGO intermediaries.

Box G9. Identifying procedures in urban government

The first stage is to obtain approval to undertake the work (Box 1).

- Micro contracts are identified through participatory infrastructure planning.
- Preliminary cost estimates are prepared.
- Estimates are granted *administrative approval* by the Engineering Department in urban government.
- Detailed plans including surveys and designs are drawn up by the partners.
- Detailed cost estimates are prepared on the basis of these plans.
- These estimates are granted *technical sanction* by the appropriate officials in the ED.
- The work is *awarded* in accordance with one of the procedures outlined below.

In the case of *community as partial promoter*, this process can be undertaken by constituting a Project Approval Committee comprising all stakeholders, which has specific and clearly delegated authority to approve both the community's and urban government's contribution towards expenditure on micro contracts up to an agreed financial limit (Box 9).

The second stage is to select a procedure for awarding the work. Find out to which rules the concerned department of urban government operates and check to see which options are available. These rules may be national or state level and the detail may well vary from place to place within the same country. Common generic examples include the rules of the Public Works Department and the Municipal Department. The following procedures will typically be available.

- *Entrustment of Works by Negotiation*; registered organisations are entrusted to carry out the works up to a certain value (Boxes 16, 17, 18, 19, 21) This is the most flexible option and is likely to cause the least problems for the Engineering Department staff (Box 15). Rates for the work are negotiated between:
  - the micro contractor and the Project Approval Committee if the community is partial promoter;
  - the community and the Engineering Department if the community is the contractor.
- *Departmental Works* executed directly through employing daily skilled and unskilled labour from the community. Onerous for staff to supervise (Box 13).
- *Labour Contract*: the Department arranges for construction materials to be available at the site; the community group provides local labour to a micro contractor (Box 14), or alternatively becomes labour contractor (Box 15).
- *Piece work agreements and Work Orders* may be used for very small works, up to about Rs 2000-3000 at the discretion of the Engineer. May be a useful entry point but the financial limit very low for widespread adoption
- *Cooperative Societies* formed for the purposes of undertaking minor works. Government may be empowered to award a certain quota of work at a discount on the tender price. This depends on local criteria.
- Award of the work using the system of *competitive tender* (Box 3). This is unlikely to be appropriate if the community group is the contractor, due to barriers of contractor enlistment and financial capacity (Box 5).

Box G10. Cost estimation and access to finance

If the community group is either the full or partial promoter, or the contractor, it will have to:

- prepare cost estimates;
- consider access to finance;
- be prepared to enter in to negotiations.

The basis for cost estimation when government is involved is the Schedule of Rates; however, the real cost depends upon the prevailing market rates and these rates should be used to estimate the likely cost of the work (Box 6). If the *community is the promoter*, these are used as the benchmark for negotiating with the micro contractor and ensuring money is efficiently spent. The finance provided by both the community and urban government must be accessible to pay the micro contractors.

If the *community is the contractor*, the actual procurement procedure adopted determines the requirements for pricing the work and the need for finance.

Departmental Works; Labour Contract; Piece work agreements and Work Orders.

- Estimate rates for skilled and unskilled labour.

- Access to finance is not a problem; labour is paid in arrears.

Entrustment of Works by Negotiation; Cooperative Societies; Competitive tender

- Estimate cost for completing construction of the works as specified, including: all labour; purchase, carriage and storage of materials; management time including record keeping.

- Require access to finance for 'up front' purchase of materials prior to settlement of the first invoice by urban government, or an arrangement with them for advance payment to cover the 'up front' costs (Boxes 16, 17).

Box G11. Preparing to enter into agreements

Prior to entering an agreement, which may include drafting and signing a contract, it is important that all parties enter into discussions during a joint workshop to clarify a number of important issues in order to avoid misunderstandings and difficulties during the implementation. The clear message is that we are partners and want to negotiate the basic conditions of our relationships. All of the following points are crucial, whether the community is the promoter, the engineer or the contractor.

We need clarity about responsibilities.

- Use simple and clear language so that everyone understands to what they are about to agree; the outcomes should be incorporated as far as is possible.
- Clarify who will be responsible for the operation and maintenance of the infrastructure and who will own the assets created (Boxes 7, 13, 23).
- How and by whom will physical progress and quality of work be monitored and approved (Box 12).
- What are the bonuses and damages for completion before and after the contract time.
- How is the completed work to be handed over.
- How will disputes be resolved.

We need clarity about money.

- Who is paying the bills. Urban government has fixed disbursement procedures even if it is only partial financier.
- If joint financing is involved, what are the mechanisms to deal with the joint operation of the accounts. Unless clear instructions and authorisations can be agreed, avoid joint bank accounts.
- What are the mechanisms for channelling the money: submission and payment of bills for certified work; how to request an advance (if appropriate) against particular items; settlement of advances.
- Will there be compensation if the bills are not paid on time. The time required to pay a bill should not be more than 14 days.
- What are the audit and account requirements and how can they be incorporated into the process.
- Who is accountable to whom; what are the liabilities and responsibilities.

We need clarity if a contract is involved.

- All signatories must understand what they are signing for.
- Who are the parties to the contract.
- What are the sole and joint responsibilities of the parties involved.
- What will be the value of the contract.
- What will be the duration of the contract.
- What securities are required and why; this could include personal securities, but wherever possible do not ask for earnest money and performance guarantees.
- How can the partners terminate the contract and for what reasons.
- Who will actually sign the contract and under what delegated authority.
- Are the parties clear about the enforcement of the contract; is it to be court ordered or private ordered.

Box G12. Selecting a contract type

- *Legal contracts* are designed to be enforced by court ordering and need to be used if urban government is involved.

- *Relational contracts* rely on self-enforcement or 'private ordering'.

This leads to several options:

- *Verbal contract:* generally the mode in the informal sector; also common in formal sector sub-contracting. If *Specified,* there is a mutual verbal agreement between the stakeholders. If *Unspecified,* there is no specific verbal agreement, but an understanding exists between the stakeholders as to their expected roles.

- *Written informal contracts:* a simple legal contract, for example as used in Departmental Works in SKAA Pakistan. (Box 28)

- *Written formal contracts:* typified by the standard contracts used by urban government in the tender contract method of procurement. Non-standard conditions may be tailored to the requirement of the different stakeholders.

Whether legal or relational contracts are used, it is important to ensure clarity with respect to roles and responsibilities.

- Are the contractors literate or do they have the access to somebody who could read and translate the documents? If yes, a written contract could be used; if no, contract conditions must be specified verbally.

- Are the potential contractors used to working with any particular type of contract? If yes, consider building on the existing practices.

- Is the contract likely to be enforced by court ordering? If no, an informal contract could be adopted; if yes, either legal assistance may be required or in the case of urban government standard contracts and conditions can be used.

Box G13. Negotiating a contract

It is customary that the promoter specifies or drafts the conditions of contract; the contractor is asked to work as per the contract conditions. In the case of partnering, the conditions of contract need to be used as a working document. The following issues need to be discussed between the partners during negotiation regardless of the type of contract to be adopted.

- Definitions as appropriate: terms such as 'Engineers', 'Contractors' and 'Clients' need explanation in the context of the contract.

- Intentions of the partners.

- The contract documents.

- The contractors obligations.

- The employers duties.

- Commencements and completion.

- Defect liability.

- Control of the works.

- Employers Instructions.

- Variations.

- Sureties and advances.

- Payments.

- Statutory Obligations.

- Injury to persons and property; indemnity to Employer; Insurance.

- Settlement of disputes: reference to the law in the case of court ordered contracts.

Box G14. Documentation

The requirements of the documents are determined by the type of contract used. Obviously in a verbal contract, no documentation is involved. On the other hand a formal contract may involve a whole variety of documents. The obvious but nevertheless key point is that they must be comprehensible to all the partners involved.

The documents can be classified according to the stage of the contract.

- Before the contract is awarded including the tender documents.

- Documents that become part of the contract.

- Documents used in managing the contract.

- Documents used in closing the contract.

A typical formal contract contains the following documents:

- Instructions to the potential contractor.

- Conditions of contract.

- Specifications.

- Bill of quantities or schedule of rates or reference to those.

- Form of agreement.

- Drawings and plans.

- Sureties and insurance requirements, if any.

- Mechanism of evaluation of the tender or offer.

Preparing Documents

- Keep the language simple and clear. One or other party may not be literate and have no legal background. If the chances of going to a court of law are remote (as is the norm in micro contracts), do not write the contract solely for the purposes of litigation.

- Are the documents clear enough for a community group to reasonably cost the works and services for which it is bidding.

- Are the documents compatible with the custom that the local micro contractors and artisans are used to working with. For example, they may only be familiar with bidding on a percentage rate basis.

- Give the contract documents a managerial function, including communication of what is to be done (Boxes 6, 7, 26 – 30).

Box G15. Sample form of agreement

Note that in cases involving urban government, whilst it is theoretically possible to have simple documentation, we have found that in practice it usually resembles that used as a matter of course in routine procurement (Box 27, 29). The form of agreement can be very simple, as the conditions of contract can form a separate document. For contracts not intended primarily for court ordering the language of the form can be tailored to local custom and language. However, in many government departments, the forms are prescribed.

THIS AGREEMENT is made on [date] between [Name of a partner] and [other partner/s].

The partner [Name of the partner] will act as [Role] and partner [Name] will act as [Role].

The addresses of the partners are as follows: [List the complete addresses and contact numbers if any].

WHEREAS it is mutually agreed between the partners to carry out the following [Briefly describe the work].

The contractor shall perform and complete the work/service for the payment made by the Client within [mention contract duration]. The work shall be carried out according to the [refer to the conditions of contract]. The following documents are part of the contract [list the documents, if any].

SIGNATURES OF THE PARTNERS with full names.

SIGNATURES OF TWO WITNESSES

Box G16. Managing community partnered micro contracts

The right atmosphere
Government officials are likely to be challenged and questioned by the community, which may engender some anxiety in the officials. In any novel process, all partners need support and training; an atmosphere of mutual respect and support is required which allows for flexibility as there are no hard and fast rules of management. As we have seen in Sri Lanka, good working relations can develop between community groups and officials, with empowerment through the assumption of power and the delegation of authority. Officials have and could trust community partners in a way they do not trust many of their conventional contractors.

An open ended process
This process of procurement has wider objectives than the production of goods or the delivery of services. Even though a contract has discrete start and completion dates, community development, empowerment and poverty alleviation are longer term and open ended. The impact of community partnered procurement is likely to continue after the completion of the infrastructure works. Operation and maintenance of the services is one mechanism for sustaining further involvement.

Irregular inputs
The internal resources available within a community vary from one situation to another. People are likely to be working elsewhere and may only be available during evenings or weekends. On the other hand government officials generally work regular hours. A flexible timing approach for the key officials working on community partnered procurement may be required.

Informal and formal positions
Many artisans, who may have a key role in this process, although well experienced may lack formal qualifications. Government officials are professionally qualified and formally trained people and their position attracts a particular status in society. This difference in background may put a strain on the communication channel between the two; officials need to understand the language and way of working of artisans.

Guidance not policing
A community has nothing to gain and everything to lose if it produces poor quality work; in terms of quality, there is an alignment of the goals of the community and the government officials. In a conventional situation, construction supervisors are policing the contractors. In community partnered procurement the community groups need guidance and support; thus these relatively junior officials have a crucial role at the operational level and much depends upon them and the support which they in turn receive.

Monitoring
We have found little data on the productivity even of conventionally procured construction works. It is crucial to keep good records related to community partnered contracts in order to monitor performance, continually strive for higher standards of quality, and build up a base of experience which can be used as a sound basis for future estimation.

Annex 1

Text boxes relating to community partnered
procurement of urban infrastructure.

Boxes 1 to 6 describe the conventional procurement procedures which are widely used by urban government in South Asia.

Box 1. Procurement procedure in engineering departments of urban government

This procedure stems from the Public Works Departments (PWD), and its principles are used by most government implementing agencies.

Narrative

1. Formulation of a scheme and its requirements need not necessarily be done by the Engineering Department (ED); the ED procurement procedure starts once the requirements of the scheme have been put before it, regardless of their origin.

2. Preliminary cost estimates are prepared.

3. These estimates are approved by the ED; this is termed *administrative approval.*

4. The necessary surveys, plans and designs are drawn up by the ED engineers.

5. Detailed cost estimates are prepared on the basis of these plans (Box 6).

6. These estimates are approved by the appropriate officials in the ED; this usually involves the Chief Engineer; this is termed *technical sanction.*

7. The work is *awarded;* there are a number of options available for implementing construction of the infrastructure (Box 2).

8. Completion of construction and *finalisation of work.*

9. Completion and end of the *defect liability* period.

Commentary

- In general, the basis here is 'rule of thumb' and past data.

- The basis of these cost estimates is the government approved Schedule of Rates (SoR) and approved details. PWD is the main source of reference.

- The preference is always for competitive bidding.

- Marked by the last entry of the measurement book, as reflected in the completion certificate.

Box 2. Urban government procedures for awarding work to construct infrastructure

Narrative

1. Award of the work to a private sector contractor using the system of *competitive tender* (Box 3). Tenders are usually submitted on a 'percentage plus' basis; that is, rather than fill in his own rate for each item of work, the contractor takes the engineers' estimate as per the government schedule of rates and adds on a percentage of the total. This percentage has to include his own profit, but more importantly it must also allow for the difference between the schedule of rates and the actual market rates for materials and labour.

2. *Departmental Works* in which work may be executed directly by the ED through employing daily skilled and unskilled labour. A muster roll of the labourers has to be maintained. The materials required are issued from the government store by indent or purchase directly chargeable to an authorised agent.

3. *Piece work agreements and Work Orders* are strictly 'contract types'; they are included here as they can be used for very small works, up to about Rs 2000-3000. They can be undertaken at the discretion of the Engineer and do not have to be submitted to such lengthy procedures as larger contracts.

4. *Entrustment of Works by Negotiation*; registered voluntary organisations or cooperatives engaged in 'social service' or 'local improvement efforts', or one or more 'beneficiaries of works' may be entrusted to carry out the works. The ED negotiates rates.

5. *Cooperative Societies* can be formed for the purposes of undertaking minor works. These exist in India; examples are 'unemployed engineers' and 'labour' cooperatives.

Commentary

- This is the routine method of procurement used in almost all situations.

- The wording of the items are standard; experienced contractors know what is and is not included in the SoR, and often do not consult it.

- This is now generally limited to maintenance work.

- This has very limited use. The responsible Engineer must show that adopting negotiation does not increase the cost above, that which would result from tendering, and that unusual circumstances warranted the procedure.

46

...Box 2. Continued

Narrative

In some cases the ED is empowered to award a certain quota of work at a discount which can be as much as 10 per cent off the tender price.

6. *Labour Contract*: the ED arranges for construction materials to be available at the site; the labour contractor hires the necessary labour and undertakes to carry out the work. Payment is based on the measured quantity of work carried out.

Box 3. Urban government arrangements for awarding contracts through competitive tendering

Narrative

1. ED issues a tender notice, either by advertising in the press or placing a notice on a notice board, which invites a sealed tender for the advertised works. For larger contracts, provincial government may do this on behalf of municipalities.

2. This notice specifies the earnest money deposit, security money (Box 5), estimated cost, date and time for the submission of tenders. Box 4 describes the requirements for prospective tenderers.

3. Tenders are opened at the specified date and time by the officer inviting tenders or by his authorised agent, in the presence of the contractor or their agents.

4. Tenders are serially numbered, signed by the officer opening the tenders and the rates are read out.

5. A comparative statement is prepared.

6. The tenders together with the comparative statement with the recommendations of the Assistant Engineer or Sub-Divisional Engineer or Executive Engineer are sent to the competent authority for accepting the tender. Usually the lowest tender is accepted but the lowest tender may not be accepted if the capacity of the contractor is doubted or his record of previous work is not satisfactory, or for other valid reasons. Depending upon their rank, government engineers and officials have the authority to accept tenders up to a certain amount.

7. After the tender is accepted the contractor deposits the security money.

8. A work order authorising commencement of the works is given to the contractor, and all the tender papers are page numbered and indexed.

9. A contract bond or agreement is prepared and sealed and kept in safe custody.

Commentary

- The decision is based on the value of the work. Beyond a certain value the tender has to be advertised. The advertisement has to be processed through a central body, which takes time.

- 'Tender boxes' are still used in some departments.

- A board which generally includes a representative from the accounts section is responsible for opening the tenders.

- Rejecting the lowest bidder puts the onus on the rejecting officer. The main issues is to explain why, in absence of mistakes in the contractors offer, the department should be deprived of the benefit of the lowest cost.

- The case for rejection becomes very hard to make, if it is done subsequent to enlistment or prequalification of the contractor, who is thereby deemed suitable to bid.

Box 4. Who is allowed to bid for urban government engineering works?

Narrative

Commentary

1. The ED operates a system whereby only those contractors who are *enlisted* can submit tenders.

2. The contractors are enlisted within a particular class (usually four or five) which specifies the financial limit of the works for which they are deemed competent to bid. Box 5 describes the administrative requirements.

3. The requirements of enlistment are to demonstrate capacity in terms of experience, financial credentials, tools and equipment owned, and personnel employed.

   • The requirements are demonstrated by submitting relevant documents.

4. The contractors are enlisted for a particular duration and are required to pay an enlistment fee.

5. In general if a contractor is already working in one department it is relatively easy to work in other departments. Conversely if a contractor does not perform well in one department, he can be banned from other departments. In Sri Lanka, contractors may be required to attend training courses.

   • Litigation against the department is one of the reasons for 'blacklisting' a contractor.

6. In large scale works, potential bidders are selected for the one project only; this process of *prequalification* is similar to that of enlistment.

Box 5. Administrative and financial demands made on contractors by urban government

Narrative

1. *Earnest money* (2 per cent - 3 per cent of the tender value) must be deposited.

2. A *performance bond* for small works may or may not be required. A typical bond value is 10 per cent of the contract value and it is released after the end of defect liability period.

3. *Insurance* is not usually required for small works.

4. On acceptance of the tender, the contractor has to deposit typically 10 per cent of the tendered amount as *security money* with the department. This is inclusive of the earnest money already deposited. In some cases the money is deducted from the running bills. All money is released at the end of the defect liability period.

5. *Liquidated damages* can be imposed in the event of serious time overrun.

Commentary

- No study has been carried out on the frequencies of accidents or claims for small works.

- These demands have high associated costs which may reach over 25 per cent; this can create serious problems in arranging finance. The ultimate cost of this is borne by the client; it is reflected in the tender prices.

- Generally used as a bargaining tool. Actual incidences of imposition are negligible.

Box 6. The problem with cost estimates: who uses which cost?

Narrative

1. Government engineers prepare detailed cost estimates for technical sanction.

2. These estimates have to be based on the latest edition of a Schedule of Rates (SoR) provided by the Public Works Department.

3. The SoR is updated periodically; the problem is that in practice many years may elapse between updates.

4. The cost estimates which are given technical sanction do not reflect the actual cost of procuring the works unless the SoR is up to date.

5. The market rate for doing the work is therefore nearly always greater than the engineers' cost estimate.

6. Prices tendered for work have to reflect the market rate.

Commentary

- This provides a standard basis for tendering (Box 2).

- High construction cost inflation means that the estimates rapidly become unrealistic.

- If the actual cost of a contract increases beyond a certain limit then the approval process (Box 1) has to be repeated.

- In one extreme case, the SoR was over 15 years old, with tender prices coming in at many times the estimated value.

- These estimates serve no purpose in terms of managing the work for the contractor.

Boxes 7 to 18 focus on the variety of roles played by community groups in the procurement process.

Box 7. Working without government: community as promoter

The community, a NGO and artisans work together in the Orangi Pilot Project internal works, Karachi, Pakistan.

Narrative

1. Residents collected money and paid in full for sewers along their lanes. At first this was done without any technical support from professionals.

2. Subsequently a NGO provided technical assistance in terms of cost estimation, supervision and provision of formwork. Training was provided for masons.

3. Some of these trained masons lobbied for more work in the neighbouring lanes and started specialising in similar works. They formed work-gangs and undertook a lot of lane sanitation work.

4. The rates were negotiated on the basis of the estimation provided by the NGO, which was based on the prevailing market rates.

5. The estimation gives a breakdown of the labour and material for ease of ordering.

6. The material was purchased by the community.

7. For excavation work, specialist labourers were usually hired; in some cases the work was done by the residents.

8. For concrete work, a mason was generally hired on either a lump sum or item rate-basis.

9. Maintenance was done by the residents; if the problems were simple. In the case of major problems they lobby and seek help.

10. There was no written contract involved. Disputes were resolved through 'social pressure'.

Commentary

• A genuine demand for the service already exists.

• Evidence of enterprise development.

• A system of estimation and breakdown of rates which suits its purpose; see Box 6.

• In urban communities the assumption that the user will supply the labour may not hold good. Contracting specialisation is evident.

• This leads to problems; urban government is unwilling to adopt infrastructure which it has had no part in supplying.

• 'Private Ordering' as compared to 'Court Ordering' is the preferred mechanism of dispute resolution.

Box 8. Community as promoter, government facilitates

In some internal works of the Sindh Katchi Abadi Authority in Karachi, Pakistan, a NGO and State Government act as facilitators: there is no role for urban government.

Narrative

1. The state government department with responsibility to regularise and upgrade slums initially entrusted implementation to urban government.

2. Progress was slow, the quality of the work was poor and there were problems with cost escalation.

3. A new, dynamic leader changed the way the government department worked.

4. All the lane level work is now done by the local people themselves with technical assistance from a NGO. The people finance the improvements themselves.

5. The NGO is paid by the government department for community organisation and technical guidance. For internal (lane-level work) works that is the only contribution from the state.

Commentary

• Public sector department at provincial level deals with the regularisation and upgrading of Katchi abadis.

• This is a rare instance of a public sector department experimenting with procurement procedures.

• It has formally contracted an NGO in a capacity similar to an engineering consultant.

Box 9. Community as partial promoter

The community and government are facilitated by a private consultant funded by a donor: A project management unit (PMU) was set up in the Faisalabad Development Authority (FDA) to implement an integrated development project known as the Faisalabad Area Upgrading Project (FAUP). The local PMU staff were supported by expatriate consultants appointed by the donor agency.

Narrative

1. Local infrastructure improvements are funded 50 per cent by the residents and 50 per cent through the PMU, using donor agency funds.

2. A project to construct lane sewers was identified through community meetings; community mapping was carried out.

3. Committees were formed at area and lane levels, and for the implementation of the project. The lane (about 20-40 households) is an important unit and the lane committee typically involves 3-6. people.

4. The PMU staff designed the works partly to government standards.

5. The design was discussed with the lane committee. The main problem was the high cost; residents could not afford the specification for reinforced concrete pipes required by government. Cheaper pipes having a lower standard of reinforcement were obtained from the local market place.

6. The PMU have negotiated with the local manufacturers to try to ensure certain minimum standards in their pipe production. Modifications were made to improve the standard of manholes.

7. Cost estimates were prepared by the PMU according to both the SoR and market rates. The rates

Commentary

- A conventional survey was also done as the information collected in the mapping exercise 'was not considered proper' for Engineering purposes.

- The committees are informal and are not registered societies; there is no formal mechanism for the creation and the operation of such committees.

- The OPP has lane groups of a similar size.

- The residents were adamant that the high standards were unaffordable; an interesting stand-off arose when, in effect, the residents said that if the officials insisted on using government standards there would be no project i.e. no lane sewer at all. A balance of cost and quality was the prime concern for the community; however, they did see the importance of marginally increasing the standards for manhole covers.

- Rather surprisingly, the cost estimate based on market rates was found to be cheaper than the SoR. It seems to

Narrative

reported for the approval purposes were the rates based on the government schedule.

8. The PMU established a Project Approval Committee that has to approve all FAUP expenditure on project activities. A docment entitled 'activity proposal' was put forward for approval by the committee.

9. This proposal document gives the background, cost estimates, sketches of design, and the mechanism for implementation. It also states what the project is aiming to achieve.

10. Included on the Project Approval Committee were the Municipal Engineer and officials from FDA. They expressed concern about the authority of the committee and what exactly it was empowered to do.

11. A memorandum of understanding is signed by the PMU, the lane committee and the project imple-mentation committee. Another committee comprising one PMU social organiser and one person nominated by the lane committee is proposed.

12. The project activity proposal indicates that the increase of cost is to be borne by the community but the contract indicates that the increase will be proportionately shared.

13. The actual contract duration was about one month.

14. A joint account was opened to operate the cash requirements; this

Commentary

be good practice to use more than one basis for cost estimation; the market rate gives a better idea of what the work will actually cost.

• The activity proposal document could be interpreted as consolidated file notes, equivalent to the technical sanction in the conventional govern-ment process.

• The benefits in terms of employment, income generation and enterprise development were not explicitly mentioned in the objectives of the project.

• According to government procedure, the authority for sanction and approval is vested with individual officers of a particular rank. Their question about the legality of the committee to grant approval is well founded.

• The agreement is shown in Box 30.

• No estimate was made for the duration of the project.

• This is not an official account of FDA; people were initially reluctant to put

...Box 9. Continued

Narrative

is a joint account of the PMU Social Organiser and a member of the community acting in their individual capacities.

15. The cash flow and management of the account is not recorded.

16. The labour arrangements were varied; work was done both by lane residents and (mainly) by sub-contracted labour.

17. Typical lane sewers cost RS 12,000 to 18,000; approximately 25 per cent of the cost is labour and 75 per cent materials, which were purchased from the local market.

18. There were deviations in the cost even for such small projects. The ratio of contract cost and actual cost was in the range of 1.06 to 0.94.

19. The project progress is reported to the Senior Engineer and the Finance and the Admin. Section as well.

Commentary

their money into a joint FDA account, and confidence building was necessary. The PMU staff acted as intermediaries.

• Urban communities do not do all the labour work themselves.

• This implies that from all the contracts, about Rs 10,000 for labour and Rs 29,000 for materials is circulating in the local economy; this is a significant benefit on top of those claimed in the project proposal.

• There is inherent risk involved in construction; the main reason here reflects the problem of accurate cost estimation.

• At the project level the process is transparent.

Box 10. Community as advisers

Over twenty years the Calcutta Metropolitan Development Authority (CMDA) has evolved a system which involves the communities with councillors and contractors in a variety of ways in the slum improvement schemes funded by government and donors.

Narrative

1. Project formulation involves consultation between the community, the CMDA and the Municipality about what facilities are to be provided within the budget. Clearly understood agreement is obtained before work starts.

2. The contractor is required to have a sample of his construction work (paving, pipe laying, concreting, etc.) approved by both the engineer and representatives of the community together. This sample of work becomes the yardstick against which the quality of the rest of the work can be judged. All parties, that is the community, the engineer and the contractor therefore have a point of reference against which future disagreements can be discussed and resolved.

3. CMDA places great emphasis on completion testing, for example of pipelines. Certificated testing is incorporated into the contract and it is important that the contractor knows that it will be carried out in every case. Community representatives are invited to witness the testing so that they can see that it has been done.

Commentary

- The consultation involves the community, key local politicians and the engineering department.

- The community does not have a formal contractual role.

- CMDA places and enforces quite strict requirements on its contractors. Whilst this will be reflected in tender prices, they are getting added value in the form of improved overall management of the jobs.

- The quality of work is excellent.

Box 11. Community as partial engineer

Conventional contractor working for a NGO and supervised by a community; the Clean Settlements Programme (CSPU) in Colombo, Sri Lanka

Narrative

1. External donor agency provided the funds to the NGO.

2. Cost estimates were provided informally to the NGO by the government authority.

3. The provision of funds took a long time and the price of construction increased.

4. The donor refused to pay the escalated cost.

5. The community paid the difference of about 20 per cent of the contract value.

6. NGO negotiated the contract with the conventional contractors with the assistance of the government authority. The community was consulted at every stage.

7. The conditions of contract used were similar to those of the NHDA community contract.

8. A copy of the contract document was provided to the community.

9. Community participated in the supervision of the work.

   Review of the contract between the NGO and the conventional contractor.

10. The parties to the contract are the NGO and the contractor. Reference is made to the CSPU to provide the plans.

11. The contractor to complete the works for a certain amount.

12. The work to be started within a certain time period.

13. If part of the work is found to be of inferior quality the payments would be suspended for the whole section.

Commentary

- Funding direct to the NGO.

- Informal relations existed as the NGO official was an ex-public sector official.

- The longer the procedures the larger the risk of the price escalation.

- Community as partial financiers and client.

- NGO as partial Engineer along with the public sector CSPU.

- The process was transparent.

- Community as partial Engineer.

- The CSPU as the partial Engineer.

- Emphasis on quality.

...Box 11. Continued

Narrative

14. The contractor to take the third party risk.

15. The type of contract is 'measure and pay'.

16. 10 per cent security deposit is to be released after the end of the six month defect liability period.

17. Liquidated damages would be charged at the rate of Rupees 100 per day.

18. No claim for the price escalation is permitted.

19. Any extension of the contract in the case of unavoidable circumstances is to be mutually agreed.

20. Changes to the instructions are to be in writing.

21. First bill to be submitted after 20 per cent of the work is completed.

22. Sub-contracting is possible with the consent of the client.

23. Un-satisfactory workers to be removed from the site.

24. Reference is made to labour law for payment to the labourers.

25. The contractor to provide employer provident fund payments to labourers

26. The contractor to obtain the workmen's compensation policy.

Commentary

• The risk to be transferred from the NGO.

• Standard government attitude adopted by the NGO.

• Standard provision.

• The contractor may encounter cash flow problems.

• Note the strong influence of government conditions of contract. It seems that the NGO also adopted the role of a conventional client.

• One main difference here is that although the procurement process is apparently the same, there is no requirement for registration and enlistment. This creates access for micro-contractors who work under the supervision of the CBO.

Box 12. Community and NGO monitor a large Government contract

A loan from an international lending bank was taken by urban government, who hired a well known national consultant to plan and design slum improvement work; the NGO monitored the works in Karachi, Pakistan.

Narrative

1. At an early stage, the city Mayor instigated negotiations with a well-known NGO already active in the area, who was offered a contract for monitoring the works. A contract was signed by the government department, the Consultant and the NGO.

2. The Contractor signed a contract for construction with the government department.

3. The contractor was not a resident of the area; local people were not hired by the contractor who brought his own team of workers.

4. NGO provided technical assistance to the people for lane level construction.

5. Details of the work were provided to the NGO.

6. The NGO held a meeting at which community based organisations (CBOs) and local people agreed to assist; this ensured adequate coverage, with people monitoring work in their own area.

7. The NGO provided zonal managers, with area managers from the CBOs under them. Lane residents reported to the CBOs.

8. Some lane residents received daily wages from the NGO.

9. The main contractor offered inducements to government officials so that they did not create problems on the job.

10. The work was sub-contracted out into 56 contracts, with many more sub-contracts.

Commentary

- The political dimension is important. The Mayor of the city was shrewd enough to realise that, if the local people were not involved then, the contractor would receive no co-operation from the residents.

- Contractors have mixed views on using local labour; (Box 14)

- NGO to be technically competent.

- NGO managed to get the relevant information.

- The NGO was very effective in developing a network to achieve its objectives.

- Unfortunately, this is a standard practice.

- This is normally prohibited under the terms of the contracts used, but commonly occurs.

Narrative	Commentary
11. When the work started it was soon realised that the people were watching and were aware of the basic scope and the specification of the work. Their input prevented the contractor taking short cuts.	• The works involved are clearly well within the community's comprehension.
12. The NGO had good connections at senior levels in government which they used if there were problems with junior officials.	• The political dimension was important; a CBO does not have this sort of entrée, unless there is a particularly active councillor.
13. The finished work was of good quality.	
14. The completion of the contract was slightly delayed; some claims were made by the contractor for the cost of delays caused by stoppage of the work.	
15. After the work was completed the CBO hired local people to clean the drains and do minor repairs on a regular basis.	• A sense of ownership is there.
16. During the process, people benefited from informal training in the supervision of works. Subsequently, residents from other area contacted them for help.	• Increased networking at the community level, resulting from improved skills and confidence.

Box 13. Use of departmental works practice

The Community, NGO, and state government are involved in external works in Karachi, Pakistan. Most of our cases relate to communities contributing to internal works, that is, to improvements to the infrastructure within the neighbourhood, lane or cluster. This case concerns external works, that is, the infrastructure outside the neighbourhood that is necessary to support the internal infrastructure. State government pays the full cost of the external works.

Narrative

1. Initially, the conventional tender-contract procedure was adopted.

2. The contractors were not performing to the satisfaction of the NGO who was appointed to monitor the works.

3. The state government then opted to use the departmental works procedure (Box 2).

4. Materials were purchased by the department and labour contracts were agreed through negotiation.

5. Small contractors and some local artisans were employed.

6. All the contracts were signed in the presence of the NGO and a CBO representative.

7. The contract is best described as a memorandum of understanding; no standard forms or conditions were used and documents were written in the local language.

8. The final bill was not released until the CBO and NGO were satisfied with the work.

9. The resulting quality of work was superior.

10. The cost was lower than that of conventional contracting, as the profit of the main contractor was eliminated.

11. After construction of these external works, local people have started installing internal works.

12. The work is on-going.

Commentary

• The staff of the authority are unhappy as they now have to do work which was originally done by the contractor: e.g. purchase of material and delivery to the site on time; responsibility for security of materials; responsibility for quality of the work; management of workforce.

• The overall responsibility for performance and maintenance of the works is being disputed by the different stakeholders.

• Using PWD-based enlistment of contractors and tender process.

• Despite the good quality of the work and the low final cost, officials are concerned about possible audit objections as there was no demonstrable competition.

Box 14. Community supplies labour to a private sector contractor

The use of local labour in a donor-funded programme implemented by urban government: Cochin, India.

Narrative

1. Under a contract won by competitive tender, the contractor has made use of some local unskilled labour for landfilling operations.

2. The contractor was specifically requested to do this by the Municipality (the promotor).

3. Wages paid so far amounts to Rs 2,500 in total; it is low because machine-based methods are necessary for much of the filling work.

4. Discussions are in hand about future work on formation of access ways amounting to Rs 33,500.

5. Many contractors have their own direct labour force that they keep on the books and pay even when there is no work available.

6. For the recruitment of additional unskilled labour, the contractors turn to one of the many labour agents in the area. These agents recruit on a daily basis from gatherings at known meeting places. This is, the accepted method of hiring casual labour.

7. The rates paid for unskilled labour, known locally as 'market rates', appear to be controlled by strong union activity and are always higher than the Schedule of Rates specifies.

8. Contractors are ambivalent about being required to employ labour from the community.

9. On the positive side, they believe it helps in overcoming potential and actual hostilities with the community.

10. The downside for the contractors is a concern that they cannot exercise sufficient control over the performance of the workers, "who get the job by right" especially if local organisations have strong political influence.

Commentary

- The contract was won in the normal way through competitive bidding.

- The contractor is satisfied so far with the community labour supplied.

- There is a two-way loyalty; the contractor maintains a core work force, even during lean times, which enables him to respond rapidly using workers whom he can trust to deliver. Labourers who are retained in this way are reluctant to take part in community-based works which their contractor might otherwise bid for.

- Good relations with the community are essential for completing work on time and within budget. In extreme cases the community may deny the contractor access to the site.

Box 15. Community as a labour-only contractor for government

A donor-funded programme implemented by urban government: Cochin, India

Narrative

1. In two separate communities, labour contracts between the Municipality and the Community Management Group (CMG) have been used for the formation of lanes by placing gravel fill. Material was supplied by the Municipality (the promoter).

2. Initial efforts did not produce satisfactory quality work because of lack of technical support and supervision.

3. The negotiated labour rates were lower than the current market rates.

4. A total of Rs 12,300 has gone into the communities in the form of waged labour.

5. Negotiations with the community are underway for an additional Rs 78,600 of work pertaining to cleaning and renovating the drainage system and concreting some lanes.

Commentary

• The use of negotiation is a key issue here; the communities agreed to rates below the current 'market rate', that is the rate at which unionised labour is available.

• This clearly illustrates the need for local support and capacity building, it cannot be neglected.

• This represents good value for money for the promoter which is very important for those officials responsible for adopting non-routine ways of working.

Box 16. Community as contractors for urban government (Cochin)

A donor-funded programme implemented by urban government: Cochin, India

Narrative	*Commentary*
1. A contract has been awarded by the Municipality (the promoter) to one CMG for the construction of a new septic tank.	
2. The contract was awarded through negotiation with the CMG, following a general call for tenders, whose purpose was 'market testing'.	• Negotiation plays an important role; the final price was 10-20 per cent lower than a typical contractor's tender.
3. The CMG has taken responsibility for procurement of materials and construction.	• The 'market testing' served the purpose of demonstrating value for money; however, contractors are unlikely to tender if word gets round that it is the intention to offer the contract to the community.
4. The value of the works is Rs 50,000.	
5. The major problem was in obtaining credit for materials purchase.	• The CMG was unable to secure credit for materials purchase; the problem was resolved by an official advancing a government loan taken out in his name. A commendable gesture, but clearly a risky and unsustainable approach. This problem arose because government procedure operates on a cost reimbursement basis.
6. A mason and a carpenter teamed up to provide skilled labour and construction management inputs for the contract.	• In addition to income generation, enterprise development is evident through the teaming up of a mason and a carpenter.
7. Work is in progress. Depending upon performance on this contract, work for the remaining septic tanks will be negotiated with the community. The value of the works will be Rs 385,000, with a further Rs 71,20 available for drainage related works.	
8. Difficulties arose regarding control of the work and internal accountability which need further study.	• There may also be negative impacts on the dynamics of the CMG; these need assessing.

Box 17. Community as contractors for urban government (Cuttack)

The first time a contract was awarded by government to a community management group (CMG) in Cuttack, India, was for the construction of a community latrine, an open drain and some paving. The work was financed by a donor through a Project Management Unit (PMU) in local urban government. We have abstracted a chronological series of exhibits from the project file which reveals how matters developed.

Narrative

7/5/94
Letter signed jointly by the residents of Pattapol to the Collector and District Magistrate requesting the municipality to do the improvement work.

Commentary

• Demand from the residents to start things moving is the first stage in formulating the plans for improvement.

26/5/94
Document entitled 'resolution no. 16', signed jointly by residents formalising the CMG.

2/7/94
A letter from the secretary of the CMG; the two other signatures are not clear, but a stamp pad is used by the secretary. The letter is addressed to the PMU, and 'allows the persons sent by you'(i.e. PMU officers) to do the job. It also promises to provide labour.

• The CMG establishes itself as the means of communication between residents and the government.

• The CMG is becoming much more formal.

Undated:
A letter to the PMU from the CMG expressing interest in doing the work.

• An indication that the work was to be sub-let to the CMG on a labour only basis.

14/9/94
A letter from the CMG to the Director PMU, requesting an extraordinary meeting to discuss progress. The letter was typed in English on CMG-headed paper with the names and designations of 28 office bearers (six of whom are female), a phone number, and a reference number. Copies were sent to councillors, Municipal Health Officer, Project Officer, Community Organiser, Executive Officer of Cuttack Municipality and an Architect.

• The CMG shows a surprisingly good understanding of bureaucratic needs and channels, indicating the support given by PMU officials.

23/8/95
A handwritten letter in English from the CMG to the Collector, Mayor and the Director of the PMU regarding the problems of the area and referring to the previous correspondence. Alongside the Secretary's stamp is a larger stamp with a registration number on it.

• Increasing formalities in the CMG's dealings.

...Box 17. Continued

Narrative

18/9/95

A formal letter to the Project Director PMU with proper references, signed by the president and stamped; a copy was sent to the Engineering Manager. The letter concerns a call for tenders and indicates the interest of the CMG in the execution of the work in their area. There is a reference to the 'unemployed youths of the area' as a justification to give them the construction work.

22/9/95

A letter from the CMG agreeing to execute the work; reference is made to a verbal discussion. A request is made to give details of the works, the Schedule of Rates and the contract agreement.

28/9/95

A letter from the CMG stating that the forms which were sent by the PMU were lacking some details. The CMG was requested to fill in the form in type on a non-judicial paper. Apparently, the contract was also sent.

7/10/95

A letter from the CMG challenging the PMU on its decision to re advertise the tender for the work which they have already consented to carry out. There are some criticisms on the 'Skeleton form' of the 'community contract'. It also states that the previously requested details were not sent.

17/10/95

A letter from the Engineering Manager to attend his office within 7 days for the 'perusal of the relevant' and 'signing the agreement'.

18/10/95 and 12/11/95

Letters showing the current impasse.

15/11/95

A letter from the CMG Secretary stating that they are starting the work.

Commentary

• Tenders were invited from the conventional contractor as well. From the files it is not clear as to whether they actually received the bids or not.

• This suggests that the matter has to be passed by the executive body. A verbal agreement is reached in principle without any documentation; this does not happen within conventional procedures. A relational contract is developing.

• The CMG was sent the forms of contract to be signed without giving them any details. These they demanded. For them, dealing with the Government seems a serious business. Nevertheless, it seems that the contract was already agreed; the actual documents may be formalities.

• An indication of empowerment; the CMG is no longer just a passive receiver.

• Some discomfort on the part of the Engineering Manager, who is being questioned by the CMG.

...Box 17. Continued

Narrative	Commentary
7/12/95 A letter from the CMG requesting design changes.	• A verbal deal was struck to resolve the impasse.
14/12/95 A letter from the CMG demanding confirmation of the changes.	• The PMU created a precedent by permitting cash advances to be paid to the CMG (compare Box 16)
14/12/95 A separate letter claiming for the resulting additional expenditure.	
Undated A note from the CMG on the number of the beneficiaries of the community latrines in terms of gender.	• The CMG is involved in some form of monitoring and evaluation.

Box 18. Communities as contractor and manager for 150 government contracts

During the late 1980's the National Housing Development Authority (NHDA) of Sri Lanka pioneered a system known as community contracting. The NHDA promoted the development of Community Development Councils (CDC), through which the program operated. This remains one of the most important programs of its kind anywhere.

Narrative

1. The CDC identified community requirements with the NHDA and sometimes NGO support.

2. Over a three year period 150 contracts were awarded. 65 were awarded to 27 communities; 32 per cent of the contracts were awarded to two particularly active communities.

3. Most of the work involved sanitation and water supply.

4. Some communities provided labour themselves whilst others hired it in through informal subcontracts.

5. 93 contracts between 1986-89 amounted to RS 4.7 million, of which about RS 1.7 million was for labour.

6. The quality of work was good; the cost was about 20 per cent less than conventional contracting, with less than 10 per cent of contracts overrunning their cost.

7. NHDA engineers and accountants had reservations about this approach.

8. The CDC's experienced problems in obtaining advance payment.

9. The Municipal Council is officially responsible for maintenance.

10. It is not clear to what extent the NHDA schemes are actually having maintenance works carried out or by whom.

Commentary

• CDCs have legal status, equivalent to that of an 'approved registered society', to undertake specific works.

• Making such choices are themselves experiences in empowerment.

• Both waged labour money and the money used for the local purchase of the materials is injected into the local economy. This has an important impact on the local market for building materials.

• The time performance was not as good as the cost and the quality. There was no systematic method to determine the contract duration.

• Questions were asked about the legality of the contracts and the lack of formal accountability in the process adopted. In some cases the CDC managed to obtain finance privately. The officials also co-operated in advancing the money before the work was completed. This was a risk, as cost reimbursement is made on certification of completion.

• The Municipal council has not adopted the system of community contracting.

Boxes 19 to 26 focus on process and contracting issues involving the community in the procurement process.

Box 19. The community contracting process in the NHDA, Sri Lanka

Narrative
Contracting process

1. Drawings approved by the Deputy General Manager (DGM), Engineering services, generally signed on the Drawing.

2. Estimates approved by the Manger Quantity surveying.

3. On query from Divisional secretary, a list of potential community contractors is provided.

4. Quotation and consent called from the recommended community contractors.

5. Contractor is selected.

6. Approval for the contract award is taken from the NHDA Chairman.

7. Letter of award.

8. Contract is signed.

9. It generally takes 3 months from preparing the drawings to the signing of the contract.

Billing process

10. Technical officer helps the contractors to prepare the bill and measurement sheets.

Commentary

• Equivalent to the technical sanction in works procedure of PWD.

• Same as above.

• CDCs are selected in consultation with NHDA. The implication is that a list of the potential community contractors is available.

• If the contractor is from outside the community, quotations are called for.

• The most senior official in the organisation approves the contract award. This may be because the lower level officials are not confident about the legality of the procedure they are adopting.

• Very similar to the PWD procedures. The main difference is in the selection of bidder and the contractor, non-conventional contractors and negotiation.

• Lead time for signing the community contract.

• Officials supervise preparation of the Bill. This could reduce the time taken in checking.

...Box 19. Continued

Narrative	Commentary
11. Measurement sheet signed by the technical officer and the Contractor's representative.	• Joint measurement for the 'measure and pay' approach.
12. Engineer checks, signs and sends to the Quantity surveyor (QS).	
13. QS checks and sends back to the Engineer.	
14. Engineer recommends it and sends it to DGM Engineering.	
15. DGM approves it and sends it to the DGM Finance.	• For payment the bill does not go higher than the DGM (approximately five steps).
16. DGM Finance processes the bill which is then paid	
17. It takes about one month from the Technical officer preparing the bill before the payment is made.	• Bill processing time.
Some comments by NHDA officials.	
18. There is now not much difference in the supervision time for the conventional contractor and the community contractor.	• Initially it took much more time to handle community contracts. *Now that there is an operational system in place, there is no significant difference in the management of conventional contracts and community contracts.*
19. Community contractors experience cash flow problems; they wait for the payment before proceeding to the next stage	
20. The work is in some cases subcontracted out. The labourers are, in general, from the community but skilled workers come from outside. Daily rates for skilled and unskilled labour were Rs 250 and Rs 150-200 respectively.	• Bill processing time is an important consideration for payment to the small contractors as they do not have much working capital.
21. Generally, materials are bought locally, but in case of shortages it may be issued from the government stores.	• Income generation.

• Circulation of money in the local area. |
| 22. Officials think that CDC makes more than 15% profit and invest in some businesses. | • Enterprise development and making a profit is important for sustaining the activities. |

Box 20. The Government of Sri Lanka reviews and assimilates community management and contracting

This Box is based on a review of a series of letters between officials of the Ministry of Housing, Construction and Public Utilities and the Ministry of Finance during 1995. It is particularly interesting because it reviews and questions the whole concept of community based procurement in an open and non-perjorative fashion.

Narrative

1. A large scale enquiry by the Treasury was held to 'review the entire system of negotiated contracts to societies' Their main concerns were:

   - 'the public funds are squandered by the interested parties';
   - lack of transparency.

2. All government organisations who have used the system were asked for:

   - the upper limit value of the contracts;
   - types of work suitable for this approach;
   - defining the capability of the societies.

3. NHDA responses centred on:

   - The system is effective in utilisation of local and foreign funds.
   - The community contract is a key tool for community participation.
   - The system was internationally acclaimed.
   - Their systems have been audited and 'have not revealed any adverse comments'.
   - The benefits are; speed, quality, user satisfaction and the 'benefits of profits being passed to the user communities'. The shorter delivery time was also emphasised.

4. The action proposed to improve the situation is to register the societies and to take their capabilities into consideration.

Commentary

- These enquiries should be seen in a positive light. The government is not seeking to abandon the practice but to overcome its shortcomings. Their concerns are perfectly reasonable.

- There is a will to assimilate the on going process by moulding it into a shape which fits the public sector processes.

- Key points in the defence are: a means to meet wider objectives which is not afforded in conventional contracting; the system has a good reputation.

- Getting the initiatives audited has turned out to be an advantage.

- A clear understanding of the benefits of the system. It is not only the construction time but time including preparation time for the contract.

- The capacity of the community is an important consideration. Mechanisms are required to evaluate that capacity.

...Box 20. Continued

Narrative

5. A committee of technical and administrative staff was appointed to recommend to the Divisional Secretary which societies should be enlisted.

6. The list of registered societies is to be made available to all Government institutions.

Commentary

•   Equivalent to the registration of conventional contractors.

•   The enlistment only needs to be done by one government body; Societies can then undertake work from more than one department.

Box 21. Government of Sri Lanka formally recognises community management and contracting

Based on a review of the following Treasury circular letters
No. Finance 227 dated 1984.
No. Finance 255 dated 1988.
No. Finance 322 dated 1993.
No. Finance 345 dated 1996.

Narrative

1. The subject of the correspondence is the award of small scale contracts to:

   • rural development societies, Gramodaya mandalayas and similar societies;
   • multi purpose and labour Co-operative Societies,
   • approved societies;
   • organisations in former irrigation schemes.

2. The government had earlier approved some organisations to undertake work; e.g. School Development Boards (up to Rs 1 million) and youth clubs affiliated with Youth Services Councils (up to Rs 37,500).

3. An exemption is granted to approved societies, which can award small scale construction work on a negotiated basis without resorting to public tender procedures. Number of contracts is restricted to four per society with a total cost of Rs 1.0 Million.

4. The work is not awarded to the society for works 'outside the area of authority'. 'Where the area of authority is not defined the Divisional Secretary of the area should be regarded'.

5. The Committee on Public Accounts noted that in order to enable approved societies to take on as much as possible, major jobs had been split into smaller parcels in order not to exceed the upper financial limit. The Ministry communicated its concern on this matter.

Commentary

• The circulars are signed by the Deputy Secretary to the Treasury.

• Provisions are made to enter into contracts with legally approved societies.

• *This is a crucially important waiver offered to approved societies*

• Confidence in the societies has increased. Previously the limit was Rs 750,000.

• Note that the society is not restricted to the locality where it exists. In some cases it may be the whole division, but they act within a defined jurisdiction.

• This emphasises that the use of public money is open to scrutiny, and that there are 'watchdogs' whose duty it is to draw attention to procedural irregularity of any sort. The underlying assumption is

Narrative

6. The approved societies must 'provide all necessary superintendence during execution'.

7. There is a strong emphasis of reporting on the physical and financial targets of the works.

8. 'Concession .... does not dispense with the requirement of the executing agencies having to enter into a *formal contract*'.

9. 'Undertaking of *negotiated contracts.....does not* debar any approved societies from tendering for other projects'.

Commentary

that 'unpackaging' of contracts is not appropriate; conventional wisdom is that there are economies in procurement if the opposite occurs, i.e. packaging of many small contracts into one larger one.

• There is a difference in how the contractor is selected, here by negotiation, and the way the contract is formed; it remains a formal contract.

• This effectively permits the societies to become 'conventional contractors'. On the other hand the conventional contractors may also become 'approved societies' and get the work without tendering. There is no mention that the provisions are only for poor areas. Negotiated contracts with the approved societies are supported by the circulars.

Box 22. NHDA Guidelines for community management and contracting

The NHDA issued the following Guidelines for assigning small contracts to community organisations. They were written in Sinhala for NHDA District Managers for use in the '100 Homes Programme', which is a new low profile initiative for delivery of shelter on the basis of electoral area.

Narrative

1. Reference is made to Financial Circulars of 1987 and 1993. Further details can be obtained from the Deputy General Manager (DGM) Engineering Services.

2. Before assigning the contract, plans and estimates must be approved by the DGM and the Officer for Financial Grants.

3. Construction should be on 'land legally undertaken by the Housing Authority' and should be 'technically certified for suitability for consumption [i.e. usage]'.

4. Priority is given to the registered society of the colony. If no such organisation is available then one can be selected from outside the area by the regional tender board.

5. The society should show written consent to accept to contract according to the respective plans, conditions and estimated cost.

6. The document should be signed by the President, Secretary and Treasurer of the society, and then by NHDA District Manager.

7. A sample letter for the award of a contract is shown.

8. The letter assigning the contract (i.e. the work order) must have:

   • Contract number.
   • Name of contract.
   • Value of contract.
   • Required date of completion.
   • District Manager's signature on behalf of NHDA.

Commentary

• The basis of the procedures is clearly mentioned.

• Equivalent to Administrative Approval and Technical Sanction (Box 1).

• Equivalent to planning permission.

• There is a clear requirement for the society to register in order to acquire the legal status necessary to enter into a contract. This clarifies the legal status of the Society.

• Emphasis is on written acceptance with clear reference to the nominated office-bearers of the Society.

...Box 22. Continued

Narrative

9. The Society has to give its written consent to undertake the contract.

10. The contract has to be signed before the start of the work.

11. There is a provision for damages due to delays equivalent to 1/1600 of the value of the work daily.

12. 15 per cent is allowed in the estimates as institutional expenses or profit for the registered society.

13. The original of the signed contract is kept by the NHDA District Manager.

14. On the contract original, a postage stamp should be attached and signed. The value of the stamp should be proportional to the contract value; 1 rupee for every 100 of the contract value. A 10 rupees stamp should be used for the contractor's copy.

15. Copies are provided to the Contractor, DGM NHDA, Auditor General, District Accountant and the District Engineer.

16. Each copy of the contract agreement should have the following attached:

    • appendix of the agreement;
    • letter awarding the contract;
    • letter of consent from the Society;
    • estimates signed by officials of the society.

17. Every contract assigned by the District Officer must be listed in a general ledger.

Commentary

• It is not clear who is offering and who is accepting. It appears that the work order is accepted once the Society formally agrees internally.

• The profit element is formalised.

• This serves the function of a revenue stamp; there is no distinction made between the revenue and the postage stamp.

• These are the 'concerned persons'.

• The requirements are very formal in nature.

Box 23. A more complex process involving the community, NGO and a Governmental project unit

The contracting arrangements in the programme of the Clean Settlements Project Unit (CSPU) in Sri Lanka involve three parties, and are revealed by following the process for financing and billing for work.

Narrative

1. Applications to formulate a scheme come from the Divisional Secretary (state government) to the CSPU.

2. Feasibility study is done by the CSPU.

3. Site is selected.

4. The applicant is informed; a copy is sent to Divisional Secretary.

5. 'Support organisations' (SOs) are identified; CSPU selected 6 out of a list of 300 for phase 1 pilot projects.

6. Agreement signed with the SO.

7. SO starts mobilisation and makes an assessment of the capacity of the community.

8. A community action planning workshop is organised by SO and CSPU to work out the needs of the community.

9. SO prepares plans for relevant activities to be included in the project proposal.

10. CSPU makes initial cost estimates.

11. CSPU, through SO initiates advocacy, and collects the 20 per cent financial contribution from the community.

Commentary

• The community has to go through the Divisional Secretary.

• There is no mention of involvement of the CBO up to this point. It is assumed that the application has come as a result of such involvement.

• SOs are not necessarily just the NGOs but include a variety of organisations who have relevant resources to offer.

• The contract is between the SO and the CSPU.

• Signing contract with the SO and site selection are concurrent.

• Emphasis on use of the workshops.

• This is one of the first documents in the payment files of the assignments. It is similar to the 'project activities proposal' in FAUP (Box 9). The difference here is that, apparently, the SO does the workshops rather than government. Experience gained in the NHDA programme was used.

...Box 23. Continued

Narrative   *Commentary*

12. The other project components (health, education, social development) start.

13. Detailed designs and cost estimates are prepared.

- Equivalent to the technical sanction.

14. The CBO lodges its contribution in their bank account.

- CBOs have to have the bank account. They link into the formal sector. There is experience in such practices from previous NHDA programmes.

15. On receipt of money the assignment (Contract) is signed by the three parties.

- The documents are prepared but signed only when the money is received.

16. Award letter issued to the CBO.

- Similar to public works procedures.

17. If required, a mobilisation advance of 20 per cent of the estimated cost can be made. The SO may arrange the bank guarantee, which is necessary in most cases.

- Is this what is supposed to happen? Is the SO capable and willing to arrange the bank guarantee? The requirement for a bank guarantee indicates that for the CBO an important barrier remains. It subsequently appears that the SO provided a note of reference rather than a bank guarantee. The advance given by the community was viewed as a cash guarantee.

18. Work starts.

19. Technical officers of the SO assist in obtaining materials, in preparation of bills and day to day management.

- This role is parallel to that played by the officials and OPP in the case of SKAA direct labour (Box 13, 25) and in NHDA (Box 19). The officials also played a similar role in community contracting in NHDA. The role of the NGO is that of partial Engineer and partial Contractor.

20. CSPU staff provide top level supervision and problem resolution. They also lay out the work and provide the levels.

- The SO could not perform all of the technical functions. Note the laying out of work and levels are done by the CSPU. Another tier of supervision; at what cost and benefit?

21. CBO have not so far subcontracted any work, but it is

- No restriction on sub-contracting empowers the CBO.

Narrative

permitted. They provide labour from within communities or hire usually skilled labour from outside.

22. CBO submits the bill which is checked and signed by the SO.

23. CSPU Engineering staff verify the measurement sheets and 'measure and pay'.

24. A percent retention is kept but the amount is not to exceed 5 per cent of the contract amount.

25. Completion is not certified. They are planning to issue certificates for future works.

26. Hand over to the CBO.

27. Maintenance period, generally for six months, commences. Any defects identified in this period are to be rectified.

28. End of defect liability period and release of retention money.

29. Maintenance should be done by the CBO but there is no agreement in place, nor is a schedule of maintenance provided.

Commentary

• Role of NGO is that of engineer certifying the bills.

• Checking the SO's checking. Is this excessive? If the SO is not trustworthy or capable why give it the role?

• Very similar to conventional contracts. The bills are paid in arrears; in addition the deposit is also retained.

• Completion certificates are not yet issued but will be in the future.

• This implies that the work is not handed over to other government agencies. The CBO appears responsible for maintenance. Are they capable of it?

• CBO's retention money is kept until the maintenance period is finished. This shows that the CBO has the capacity to survive the conventional barriers of procurement, demonstrating enterprise development. The next stage is to bid against conventional contractors.

• A formal contract for maintenance was not made due to the 'temporary nature of the CSPU' who will not enter into a long term agreement. This implies that any maintenance contract has to be between permanent organisations. The project's organisations are not suitable to handle such tasks. This also points out the importance of having exit or completion procedures in the project design. There needs to be clear understanding as to which organisation is going to inherit the liabilities of the project. The organisation responsible for maintenance must exist for the whole life cycle of infrastructure or delegate such functions to other organisations.

**Box 24. Is the client getting value for money?
The cost of intermediaries**

The Community acts as partial promoter/client and partial contractor with the involvement of a NGO intermediary for the CSPU in Sri Lanka. (Also see Box 23)

Narrative

1. A service agreement is signed by the CSPU and a NGO.

2. The three phases of the project are: development, implementation, consolidation. For each phase a different contract was signed. The initial period was six months, subsequently increased to one year.

3. The functions of the CSPU and NGO are mentioned in the agreement. The two components for payment are: firstly staffing; secondly based on project outcome.

4. Two month advance payment was provided without any guarantee.

5. The NGO submits reports monthly and is paid. A 10 per cent overhead charges was agreed.

Review of project files

6. There are two types of files: contract files and payment files. The contract file deals with the stages up to the signing of the contact.

7. The contract was in Sinhala.

8. The contract value for the implementation phase was Rs.158,070.

Commentary

• Consultancy agreement with non-professional organisations.

• Contracts are based on the phase of the project and separate contracts are signed for the stages with the same NGO and for the same area.

• Parallel with the consulting services. NGO as consultant.

• Advance without the guarantee is possible to the NGO or in a service contract with the NGO.

• This includes the profit as well.

• Similar filing system as in the conventional government contracts.

• Use of local language, even when dealing with the NGO.

• The consultancy cost is **1.79 times** that of the infrastructure contract cost. Is this good value for money; what are the additional benefits given that CSPU officials are also playing role in the projects? The activities related to community development have been paid separately to the NGO. It may be that the NGO provides added value above that generally provided by conventional consultants. This is a learning phase for the projects in

...Box 24. Continued

Narrative

Commentary

which management costs are high when new processes are being explored. Nevertheless, the NGO cost associated with the implementation of contract is an important consideration.

9. A bill dated 21-05-96 shows the breakdown. Under staff costs are: salaries, travelling and NGO management. Output costs include: office rent, site office maintenance, monitoring and documentation, and NGO management at a rate of 10 per cent.

    • Quite a high rate for management from non-professional managers.

10. The contract for the project development phase was Rs.183,070 over for six months. There is no contract for the consolidation as yet.

    • The value of the contract was **2.03 times** that of the contract amount for infrastructure.

Box 25. A modified process of Departmental Works using NGO as consultants

Community acts as an agent of the NGO in supervising the works, and in some cases as a contractor for SKAA works in Karachi, Pakistan.

Narrative

1. Departmental work is used for the procurement.

2. The estimation is made on the basis of market rates jointly developed by SKAA and OPP.

3. The language is made as simple as possible.

4. The micro contractors are consulted by SKAA for the estimation of rates.

5. The work is identified in consultation with the community and the NGO. The scope is restricted to external works.

6. Either the Department or OPP makes a plan which is exchanged with the other party.

7. Estimates are prepared in consultation with the NGO. The NGO checks the design and estimates.

8. A note sheet is prepared by the Executive Engineer stating that the identification was done, estimates were prepared, and the NGO was consulted and asked for approval. A cash advance was requested. The note was sent to the Director General (DG).

9. The DG approves.

10. The file goes to the Director of Finance.

11. The Director of Finance then authorises the cash advance, without which the departmental works cannot proceed.

Commentary

• An alternative to competitive bidding.

• This is a deviation as the rates used are not the government approved schedule rates.

• The line items in the bill of quantities have been simplified.

• The rates were developed in consultation with contractors.

• Plans are made with the community.

• Close working of NGO and department.

• Estimates are approved by the NGO, whose role is that of a consultant. The public sector empowers the NGO.

• 'Note sheet' is the tool of communication between the officials.

• The DG's approval is an important safeguard.

• The Finance Department provides money as an advance to the Executive Engineer. This is critical in departmental works. Payment is made before the work is done, unlike the contracting system where the work is done before payment is

Narrative

Commentary

made. The advance is internal, and the Engineer is responsible for all the further disbursements.

12. SKAA officials and the NGO enquire whether the community can do the work. If not, local micro contractors are used; Officials negotiate the price.

- Community is given the choice. A potentially complex role as commu- nity contractor, or as partial contractor and partial consultant or as manage- ment contractor.

13. In the agreement the mode of payment to the contractor is specified, usually involving staged payments .

- Personal verbal communication is important. Negotiation is the key.

14. The material is supplied to site by the department.

15. Payment for materials is made through a bank draft.

- Payment is an important issue to be specified in the contract.

16. Once the material reaches the site, the contractor starts the work.

17. After the work is completed and tested the final payment is made to the contractor.

- Procuring material is a departmental responsibility which may cause problems in co-ordination, and involve hidden costs in terms of time and money for those involved. This in effect is labour-only contract.

Boxes 26 to 30 look at the different forms of agreement and contract which have been used in cases of community partnered procurement.

Box 26. Conditions of contract for community construction contracts with NHDA Sri Lanka

Narrative

1. The contract is in Sinhala, the local language.

2. Parties to the contract are mentioned along with their addresses.

3. The President/Chairman, Secretary and the Treasurer are signatories on behalf of the community development council. The General Manager is signatory on behalf of NHDA.

4. There are spaces for two witnesses to sign.

5. A summary sheet provides the following details.
   - compensation for delays.
   - Work to be started within 14 days of the contract.
   - Defect liability period.
   - 10 per cent security deposit to be deducted from the running bill but limited to 5 per cent of the contract sum. 50 per cent of the security is to be released on completion of work and the remainder at the end of the defect liability period.
   - Period for completion of contract.
   - Type of contract is 'measure and pay'.
   - The time limit for certificate of payment is 28 days.

6. There are in total 12 clauses.

7. The scope of works and obligation of the contractors is mentioned in the first paragraph.

Commentary

- A very obvious point often overlooked by professionals.

- Standard drafting practice.

- Three office bearers sign on behalf of the contractor.

- Standard practice.

- A useful way to provide an abstract, with relevant details on one page.

- Security deposit remains part of the process.

- Contract period is specifically mentioned.

- To expedite payments and programme the cash flow.

- Very concise

- Standard drafting practice

...Box 26. Continued

Narrative	Commentary

8. Clause 1. Obligations of NHDA includes: funding, provision of plans, provision of technical advice and assistance to the construction committee for implementation.

• Clear definition of the client's tasks.

9. Clause 2. Refers to the agreed estimates and states the commitment from the contractor to complete the proposed work accordingly. Payments are to be made on the basis of a bill. The method of payment is 'measure and pay'.

• Contract is based on the negotiated rates. Disbursement is similar to conventional contracts.

10. Clause 3. Records to be kept by the committee and made accessible to the client.

• Keeping good records is important to maintain transparency and accountability and good management.

11. Clause 4. Plans and instructions given as the basis of implementation.

• Instruction and personal communication is important and cannot be replaced only by documents.

12. Clause 5. Material purchase, storage and record keeping are the responsibility of the construction committee.

• Clear definition of the tasks of the contractor.

13. Clause 6. The committee must employ trained and suitable workers and keep records of the workers and their wages.

• Emphasis on quality and accountability.

14. Clause 7. Duration of the contract.

15. Clause 8. The committee must follow the instruction of the client.

• Importance of instructions is emphasised.

16. Clause 9. The president/chairman, treasurer and two other members of the construction committees are liable for: loss of funds or materials, stoppage of work, delays and similar events. If the project is not completed the supply of funds and other services to that area will be stopped.

• Point of liability is defined. This is somewhere between personal and the organisational liability. In conjunction with clause 12, it seems the liabilities are on organisations and not on individuals.

...Box 26. Continued

Narrative	Commentary
17. Clause 10. The third party insurance and workmen compensation insurance to be provided. The cost of insurance is to be reimbursed to the contractor.	• Insurance is required and paid by the client. One option is for the insurance to be arranged directly by the client.
18. Clause 11. Breach of contract would result in termination of the contract.	• The contract is 'self -enforcing'.
19. Clause 12. Clarification that the agreement is ex-officio.	• The legal implications are that the contract is between the organisations represented by the signatories. The contract will not be affected if an official is replaced by another official.

Box 27. The community construction contract in Cuttack, India.

Narrative

1. The signatories are the secretary of the CMG and the Engineering manager of PMU.

2. The title of the work was given and reference was made to the drawings, specifications and the conditions of contract.

3. Stamped paper is used; there is a stamp of 'stamp vendor, D.S.R office, Cuttack' on the back of the agreement form.

4. The CMG supplies the materials, executes the work and maintains the work for a required period.

5. The payment is based on the item rates calculated from the Schedule of Rates.

6. A witness also signs the documents.

7. A Purchase committee is constituted by the PMU to buy materials; the President and the secretary of the CMG are to be the members.

8. The quantity of work done is to be measured.

9. Security money of up to 10 per cent of the value of the work may be deducted at the discretion of the officer-in-charge of PMU.

10. The maintenance or the defect liability period is three months; the defects are to be rectified by the CMG or the security money will be forfeited.

11. Employment of persons less than 12 years of age and giving wages less than the government minimum is prohibited.

Commentary

- A formal note is struck, following the lines of a typical engineering department contract .

- This involves making cash advances to the CMG; this creates a special case for CMGs as contractors.

- It is important to strive for internal transparency.

- Measure and pay

- Maintenance beyond the defect liability period is not addressed

- Standard clause reflecting national laws

...Box 27. Continued

Narrative

12. The officer in-charge of PMU can enquire and decide in case of complaints related to the payment of wages, quality of work and other matters.

13. The CMG must furnish proper accounts.

14. A Schedule of Rates and some sketches are attached.

Commentary

• His decision is binding and there is no reference to arbitration.

• It is not clear whether these are to be certified by the PMU or a third party. They are important for transparency and accountability both internally and externally.

Box 28. The contract used in the Departmental Works of SKAA

An example of a simple contract used for work in Zia-ul-Haq Colony in Karachi, Pakistan.

Narrative	Commentary
1. The contractor is named, along with his national identity number and the name of his father.	• A certain formality is introduced.
2. Plain paper rather than stamp paper is used.	• The contract is akin to a simple memorandum of understanding.
3. The contract is hand-written and in the local language.	• No separate conditions or specifications are provided or referred to.
4. The scope of work is mentioned; excavation, laying of pipes, jointing and testing.	
5. The rates are 'per running foot'.	• Use of item rates.
6. There are separate rates for valves and bends.	
7. The payments are staged and related to the percentage of the work completed. A fixed payment of Rs. 7,000, is mentioned on completion of 25 per cent of the work.	• Payment is related to the physical progress.
8. Testing is mentioned as a separate item	• Indicates the importance attached to testing

Box 29. A contract between three parties with a NGO as the partial consultant and partial contractor

The CSPU in Sri Lanka uses a more complex three party contract involving the CSPU, the community and a NGO.

Narrative

1. The contract is in English.

2. The term used is 'agreement for community assignment'.

3. Parties to the contract are mentioned along with their addresses.

4. There are three parties in the contract The CSPU is the first party, CBO is the second and NGO is the third.

5. A list of activities of the third party is included as an Annex. These include identification of the staff of the second party, supervision, assisting the community, acting as guarantor, keeping in contact with CSPU to solve problems, preparation of proposals, entering into the agreement, providing technical advice on behalf of the first party and 'other duties and functions'.

6. The President/Chairman, and the Treasurer are signatories on behalf of the Community Development Council. The Director is signatory on behalf of CSPU.

7. There are spaces for two witnesses to sign.

8. There are, in total, 19 clauses.

9. The name and addresses of the parties are mentioned. Reference is made to the project, community proposal and 'assistance' of the third party.

Commentary

• The contract may have been translated later.

• An attempt to make it apparently different from a conventional contract and the NHDA community contract.

• Standard drafting practice.

• Each signatory represents their organisations. It is not a personal contract.

• The third party acts as an agent of the first party to control the second party. These activities are very difficult to cost. The relationship between the first and the third party is governed by another contract. What advantage is gained by writing an agreement with three parties?

• Two representatives sign on behalf of the contractor.

• Standard practice.

• More complex than the NHDA community contract.

• Standard practice.

...Box 29. Continued

Narrative

10. Clause 1. Obligations of the first and second party: the duration, the remuneration for work and completion of the assignment by the second party. The relationship is between the first and the second party only.

11. Clause 2. Refers to billing: the third party will help the second party. Reference is again made to the community proposal, but it is clarified that the payment would be based on measurement.

12. Clause 3. Billing is to be done by the second party and the first party is to pay 'within fortnight'.

13. Clause 4. Standard clause for the retention and release of security deposit. 10 per cent is deducted from the running bill but this must not exceed 5 per cent of the total. 50 per cent is released upon completion of construction.

14. Clause 5. Refers to a separate contract for payment for services to the third party by the first party. There is no direct mention of such payments in this contract.

15. Clause 6. Provides a mechanism for price escalation which exceeds 5 per cent. The reference date is the date of contract signature and the evidence is the receipts for materials purchase. It is implied that the labour cost escalation is not covered.

Commentary

• Scope of the contract between the first and the second party.

• Inputs from the first party through the third party. The contract is 'measure and pay'.

• There is no mention of compensating the second party at a fixed rate for delays in payments.

• An important barrier affecting the cash flow of the small contractors.

• Appears to be against the spirit of the three party contract. Similar to conventional contracting with the NGO as Engineer.

• This is adventurous; no other small scale contracts have allowed this. It may be the influence of ICTAD. The evidence required is not the same as for large contracts. The question of audit acceptability arises; would any retail receipt be valid or only those of government stores? So far no claims have arisen in this regard.

...Box 29. Continued

Narrative

16. Clause 7. The 20 per cent advance payment could be made against a security bond from commercial bank, insurance agency or similar security bonds provided through the third party on behalf of the second party.

17. Clause 8. Recovery of the advance is made in instalments, starting when 30 per cent (by cost) of the work is complete. Full recovery before 90 per cent of the work is complete.

18. Clause 9 and 10. The maintenance period, and the obligations of the first party. No involvement of the third party. 2.5 per cent of the retained security will be released at the end of the period. If the second party defaults in not fulfilling the requirements, the first party may get the faults rectified at the expense of the second party. The criterion to be fulfilled is the 'satisfaction of the first party'.

19. Clause 11 and 12. Work to be completed in the time prescribed. If the second party cannot get an extension to the contract the first party can impose the liquidated damages on the second party at the prescribed rate. The limit of the damages is 5 per cent of the total value.

20. Clause 13. The project organisation. The construction sub-committee has members from CSPU, CBO and NGO. Technical advice is provided by the first party. There is an option to provide such advice through the third party.

Commentary

- Options included the NGO arranging a bond on behalf of the CBO. One NGO reported that this was beyond their capacity. There has to be a realistic alignment of capacity.

- Gradual recovery helps cash flow management. It is akin to an interest free loan to the contractor.

- There is no description as to the kind of maintenance or rectification required.

- The clock starts from the letter of acceptance. This presents a barrier if it is imposed. It seems unlikely to be invoked.

- Similar to NHDA project organisation with an addition of the NGO.

...Box 29. Continued

Narrative

21. Clause 14. Appropriate insurance cover to be provided by the second party. The cost of insurance is to be reimbursed by the first party. The first and the third party are to be fully indemnified.

22. Clause 15. The second party must maintain transparency; this clause holds them responsible for consulting the community.

23. Clause 16. The second party is responsible to 'duly maintain daily accounts, inventories, stock books, attendance registers and reports' which are accessible to the first party.

24. Clause 17. Termination of the contract with the 'consent of all the three parties' or in case of breach by the second party, the first party could terminate the contract and pay for the work completed 'only'.

25. Clause 18. In case of disagreement in the interpretation of the contract, the Secretary of the Ministry is the final authority.

26. Clause 19. ICTAD conditions are to be inferred where 'this agreement is silent'

Commentary

• The cost is ultimately borne by the client. The risk is transferred to the insurance by the first party. Not much detail is provided regarding the kind of insurance.

• This implies a difference between 'the community' and the CBO. The form of consultation (e.g. number of meetings or their outcome) is not specified. It is difficult to establish whether the contractor met this requirement or not.

• No provision for independent arbitration or conciliation.

• ICTAD conditions refer to two party contracts. It is confusing to define the NGO as a party and then to refer to the framework of a two party contract.

Box 30. The contract used in the FAUP, Faisalabad, Pakistan

This contract was used for lane sewer projects.

Narrative

1. This particular agreement is typical of several used.

2. The date of contract is 29-11-94; it is written on plain paper.

3. The implementation committee is responsible for supervision of the work. The responsibility of 'running the project' rests with the PMU social organiser and one other member of the committee.

4. The signatures were made without mentioning designations.

5. The national identification of the signatories was mentioned.

6. The stamp of FAUP is on both pages.

7. Out of six names mentioned as the neighbourhood committee only three signatures were there. There was no signature against the names of the 'supervisory committee'.

8. The signatures are generally not dated.

Commentary

• This contrasts with the 'stamp papers' used in India and Sri-Lanka. It is rather like a mutual understanding between different individuals Whilst neither standard wordings not structure are used, there is a close similarity between different agreements .

• The atmosphere seems informal; the clear message is that it is not intended to be used in the court of law.

• It is not clear who are the parties to the contract; neither are the procedural steps of 'offer' and 'acceptance' clear.

• There is overlapping responsibility with the PMU sub-engineer, who in the eyes of the government would appear to retain responsibility.

• The project duration is not mentioned.

• There is no clarity in the 'agreement' on what is to be done and for how much. It does describe what the different groups of people are supposed to do.
It is not clear whether the agreement is supposed to serve any managerial purpose.